The Long Day Wanes ...

A Memoir of Love and War

Part One & Part Two

For: Elizabeth
With love
Chester

Chester Thompson
Christmas
2006

i

Chester Thompson
P. O. Box N 3233
Nassau, Bahamas

Second Edition

Front book cover design by James Marsh—with
input by Susie Conroy and Aitken Imaging.

ISBN 0-932265-82-0

Published by

White Sound Press
379 Wild Orange Drive
New Smyrna Beach, FL 32168 USA

Voice: 386 423-7880
Fax: 386 423-7557

Also by Chester Thompson

The Fledgling

Dedication

A Cenotaph stands in a garden in the heart of Nassau flanked by the centuries old Library and Supreme Court Buildings. On its north face, nearest to the sea, are the names of those Bahamians who died in battle in World War II.

The inscription promises that they will be acclaimed by history. This book is dedicated to their memory, to add in some small measure to the promised acclaim.

The graves of some are unknown, but my research, aided by John Ansell, reveals final resting places of the following:

Flight Lieutenant (Pilot) Warren Maurice LIGHTBOURN, age 25 , in the Reichswald Forest War Cemetery in Kleve, Germany.

Flight Lieutenant (Pilot) George Winthrop Sargent MOSELEY, age 25, also in the Reichswald Forest War Cemetery in Kleve, Germany.

Flying Officer (Pilot) Joseph Basil POAD, age 21, in Padua War Cemetery in Italy.

Marine Michael MCKINNEY, age 18, in Bone on the Mediterranean coast of North Africa.

Private Carl MARSHALL, age 21, in Caserta War Cemetery, Italy.

King George V in Flanders in 1922 spoke of the war dead:

> *"there can be no more potent advocates for peace upon earth than these silent witnesses to the desolation of war."*

My sentiments include those not listed on the Cenotaph or whose final resting places are unknown to me.

In grateful memory of the Sons of this Colony who made the supreme sacrifice in World War II.

1939 - 1945
These are the men whom history will acclaim
The men who never feared to count the cost
These sons of ours who need no name
Who gave their all when everything seemed lost

PTE. A. DELEVEAUX
F/O GARTH JOHNSON
CPL GEORGE JONES
FLT/SGT WILBUR HALDANE JORDAN
FLT/LT WARREN M. LIGHTBOURN
RIFLEMAN ALFRED BURGE MALONE
PTE CARL MARSHALL

MARINE MICHAEL McKINNEY
FLT/LT GEORGE MOSELEY
PTE GEORGE MUNRO
F/O JOSEPH BASIL POAD
PTE JAMES F. ROLLE
P/O JACK SAWYER
FLT/SGT PETER STRATON

THIS WAS THEIR FINEST HOUR

THE LONG DAY WANES ...
A Memoir of Love and War

Chester Thompson's memoirs of his years growing up in Hope Town was received with considerable literary acclaim. *The Fledgling* was selected as one of the texts in the BGSCE Literature examinations for 2006 and is already established as a "must read" for those interested in Bahamian literature and social history.

Good news! Chester Thompson has put pen to paper once again and takes his autobiography from where *The Fledgling* ends to the eve of D-Day in Britain. He volunteers for the Royal Navy in early 1942. We follow him through his training in Britain and the harrowing experience of service on a destroyer giving convoy support.

These convoys of dozens, sometimes hundreds of merchant ships were hounded by U-Boats and it was the job of the destroyers to locate and sink the submarines. The loss of ships and lives was enormous and the accounts of heroism and horror are written with an understatement and reserve which intensifies the events.

We soon forget *The Long Day Wanes* is an autobiography for it is a ripping good yarn with plenty of romance and humour. There are wonderfully tender passages describing the love affair with Chester Thompson and his Annabel yet there is also barrack room ribaldry.

Chester Thompson receives his commission as an officer and the story ends while he is in intense training for the upcoming D-Day invasion of Europe. It's a bit of a cliffhanger, but don't worry: *The Long Day Wanes* is the first of two volumes. I can't wait for the second.

Jack Hardy

*****

Chester Thompson's new book tells about a young man abruptly dragged from the quiet, homespun weave of Bahamian existence into the harsh experience of life in the Great World. We meet him in the early days of World War II, when the Bahamas were a peaceful backwater to a degree we can hardly imagine now, and see him volunteer for service in the King's forces, a choice taken by no means by all the lads of that era. He is taken into the Royal Navy as a "rating," and fights his way up to receive the wavy stripes of a junior officer, having proved himself in the freezing gales, the search for the implacable German submarines, the sights of tankers torpedoed and their burning crews outlined in flames, the rescue of oil-soaked sailors, the endless round of cat-naps in sodden hammocks slung in the flooded mess-decks of tiny warships barely kept afloat.

All that relieves this grim routine are his leaves, caught between voyages, when with the young lady he comes to love he sinks into the quiet charms of rural England that, even at war, present an almost unbearable innocence. There can be no greater contrast than that between his iron-clad shipboard life and the joys of dinner in a county pub and sleep with his lady in a farm-house bedroom. We wonder how he survived the contrast without splitting in two.

The book begins with his reminiscences as a man in his eighties, when he seems to be saying that the friends he made and lost in those war times were the most meaningful in his long life and perhaps provided the fulcrum of his existence. It is the story of a Bahamian, but it is also an eternal story of any youth suddenly forced into the pain of manhood.

Richard Coulson

*****

Chester Thompson, a Bahamian from Abaco, served as an Ordinary Seaman in the Royal Navy, first on a minelayer, then on *HMS Beverley*, one of the many escort ships assigned to the convoys dodging U-boats across the Atlantic with essential supplies for Great Britain in World War II. Many of those ships never completed the long crossing.

The *Long Day Wanes* is a gripping tale of the battle of the U-Boats whose torpe-does took a deadly toll on the merchant ships until Allied aircover eventually came to the rescue, forcing Germany's Grand Admiral Karl Doenitz to admit to his diary: "We have lost the Battle of the Atlantic."

Chester Thompson lives to tell the tale because as his ship, *HMS Beverley*, was about to make her last crossing, he and a few of his mates were ordered by the Admiralty to leave the ship and report to Portsmouth Barracks for further training.

The successful three-month course led to a commission for Thompson as a Sub-Lieutenant - Royal Navy Volunteer Reserve.

But *HMS Beverley*, which had made so many successful crossings as a convoy escort, was torpedoed on April 11, 1943, with 151 lives lost.

Sixty years later, Chester Thompson still grieves for his lost shipmates, but remains in awe of his "last minute reprieve." He was meant to live to tell their story, which he does so well in *The Long Day Wanes*.

Eileen Carron, Editor/Publisher, *The Tribune*

FOREWORD

My grandchildren encouraged me to write this memoir. I was easily persuaded as I often wish that I knew more about my own grandparents and their parents.

My grandchildren are reminded of John Donne's line "no man is an island, entire of itself." In my journeys during the war, happy chance often led me to those who became good friends and smoothed my pathway.

Foremost of these were Kitty and Cecil Hart of Bramley in Surrey, my English "Mom" and "Pop," parents of Tony, my shipmate on *HMS Beverley*, "Auntie Grace" and "Uncle Hugh," the Markhams of Fordy farm in Cambridgeshire, rounded out my adopted family.

My commanding officers on ships at sea or on shore establishments invariably helped me on my way.

There are a host of others. Some will be met in the course of my narrative. The story line may not permit mention of others, of equal stature.

All accounts of the war at sea, enemy action and fierce storms are accurate. Geoffrey Blewett's informative book, *The Beverley*, was useful when memory seemed fallible. German and Allied official records are available although, in some cases, they are skewed in favor of the better known ships and officers.

With events and characters ashore, I have taken some poetic license which led to embellishment.

Chester Thompson

Big Hill
Hope Town, Abaco
July 2004

ACKNOWLEDGEMENTS

I'm indebted to those readers of my first book, *The Fledgling*, who often ask what happened next.

Their curiosity and the urging of my family have encouraged me to write of a period in my early twenties when, with millions of others, I was caught up in World War II.

My method of writing is continual re-writing. During the final transformations of my manuscript I, somewhat timorously, sought observations from the following: Eileen Carron, Paul Bower, Richard Coulson and Jack Hardy.

Their comments have enriched my book and I am most grateful. As a wartime serving officer on an escort vessel, Paul Bower's comments are particularly relevant.

I could not have completed the book so expeditiously without the computer skills of Caru Jones. My wife Joan and grandson, Thomas Phillips, helped with computer research. Joyce Waugh's typing skills were often sought. I thank them all.

The front book cover design was beautifully done by James Marsh with input by Susie Conroy and Aitken Imaging.

Attention to detail by Steve and Marjorie Dodge—and Jamie Gutierrez—of White Sound Press is appreciated.

Constraints of space will not permit mention of others, but I am nonetheless grateful.

Conversation With a Sailor

I sat by a sailor to learn of the sea,
But he swore as he drank,
Then he said to me:
Leave it alone, lad, the sea's a bitch.

all smells and bells
And bosun's yells.
The stokehole a stinkhole,
The galley a hell-hole.

'But what of the flying fish,
White moon and mermaids?
What of the islands -
Your tropical trips?'

But the sailor swore and laughed as he said,
'The sea would be fine if there weren't any ships.'

Elizabeth Beveridge

Table of Contents

Credits

"Map - Allied Shipping Losses: 1 August 1942 - 31 May 1943," and "Map - North Atlantic Convoys and the positions of Convoys SC122 and HX229 17-20 March 1943," from *The Price of Admiralty* by John Keegan, copyright © 1988 by John Keegan. Used by permission of Viking Penquin, a division of Penquin Group (USA) Inc.

PROLOGUE

Abaco

The lights begin to twinkle from the rocks,
the long day wanes, the slow moon climbs,
the deep moans round with many voices.
Tennyson

Alone on his hilltop the old man looks across the pale blue waters of the Sea of Abaco, shimmering with golden light in the afternoon sun. Nearby, the cays are clearly defined; bold brush strokes of green palms and white beaches. Known to him for a lifetime, with names like Cooper Jack, Lubbers Quarters and Tavern Cay, they seem like old friends.

Further along to the south and west the misty outline of Great Abaco Island marks where horizon and sky become one. To the east, waves surge on the reef, ending their long voyage across the Atlantic; the eternal murmur of sea meeting land as much a part of the old man as breathing. Far above in the deep blue sky several frigate birds float in slow circles. As he looks, one of these starts a steep downward spiral toward the sea. Below, white sails, as two dinghies, seemingly painted on the sea's surface, make an unhurried voyage.

Settling more comfortably in his rocking chair and closing his eyes, he thinks, "Where do I fit into this seascape? What awesome convergence of time and space placed me on this island at this moment in eternity?" Throughout his life he had been reaching out for some ultimate reality, groping for some elusive truth, seeking a clear-cut path through the tangled thickets of existence.

When he was younger it seemed he had come close to a breakthrough. Then, he could summon a pure unadulterated joy by sitting on some lonely headland, unblemished by man. There, beside the sea, where mankind's predecessors were nurtured, the meaning of life seemed almost within his grasp. In a moment the clouds would dissolve and everything would be revealed. A magic casement would open and reveal a secret world that he knew intuitively but could never visit.

It never happened and now, to his amazement, he is in his ninth decade, with a rapidly diminishing life span. Perhaps, the enlightenment he glimpsed was a mirage. Or perhaps, he thought, "it is only attainable with age: a distillation of experience; maybe from the plateau of old age I can observe the panorama of my life and see my younger self, as if I were another person, apart from myself but linked to myself."

If this is so, he thought, there is still time to record some defining events, to select from eight decades of living those episodes which might give some meaning to life; if only in the mind of a grandchild.

If this seems self-centered, so be it. What better source of the way it was than my brain with its bits and pieces of remembered experience, its cosmic mix of impressions, some of which gleam and shimmer like stray sunbeams through a cloudy sky.

There is not time for thick tomes of detail; instead, a slim volume, before "the bird flies from the lighted room into the darkness from whence it came."

The sound of a car on the driveway. Two young women step silently on to the patio and pause near the silent figure in the rocking chair.

"Grandpa is asleep," one whispers to the other, "we'll leave him to his dreams." They retreat down the stairway. There are muffled sounds as the car door is shut and it is driven down the hill.

His hand moves, a faint mischievous smile, and he retreats into the twilight that precedes sleep. This is a time for reflection, he thought; to shake the kaleidoscope of memory and see what is revealed, to summon images from that other life when he was young and his world was in the turmoil of war.

If these images are random and muddled my pen will make them sequential. The friends and foes of long ago will come on stage to tell their tales and then exit into the shadows. They will laugh and love, shout and scream; some will die, often horribly and alone, robbed of their right to grow old: frozen by the winter waters of the North Atlantic, shredded by enemy bombs in London streets, blown out of the sky over Hamburg and Frankfort. Others, more fortunate, will survive, but changed forever, living on as the world also changes.

Above his head a soft wind sighs through the branches of a madeira and the ghosts approach. Pete Lawrence, who joined the Navy at 17, always sea-sick, even in harbour; Rodney Price, revered captain; both victims, with their 150 shipmates, when the destroyer HMS Beverley was torpedoed.

Harvey 'Nick' Nicholson and Peter Walker, friends in Combined Operations, who shared the sometimes grim but often uproariously funny life in Landing Craft. As in life, they cannot conceal their irrepressible mirth.

And beyond, a ghostly throng against a background of shadowy seas. They are mostly young, as they were in life; boys and girls just yesterday, clothed in the garments of warriors. They are benign ghosts, cleansed of flaws by the years they have wandered in the labyrinthine corridors of memory. On the fringes of the throng, enemy U-boat survivors, plucked from the icy waters of the North Atlantic, have now earned clemency. He thinks, "I do not have the time or skill to direct such a large cast, so few of these will have speaking roles, but my story is their story; my story is tangled with all their stories."

And, as always, asleep or awake, he sees Annabel,

> *Most individual and bewildering ghost,*
> *A broad browed and smiling dream*
> *Move light as ever through the lightless host,*
> *Quietly ponder, pause and start and sway*
> *And turn and toss her blonde delightful head*
> *Amusedly, among the ancient dead.*
> 						*Rupert Brooke*

CHAPTER 1

1939

Nassau

The Reds and my team, The Blues, were at rugby practice on the Eastern Parade Ground. Rugby season was
eight weeks away, but we had a mission. The year before,
our common rival, the Buccaneers, clobbered both our
teams. Their final score, against The Blues, was 31 to 4. We
were humiliated and determined to get our revenge.

And now a year later, with the sun slanting into the west,
practice was going well. I had taken the ball through the
opposing forwards, heading for a touchdown, when I saw
my father, aided by his walking stick, hobble on to the field.
I slowed to a walk and went toward him, still holding the
ball. It was a dumb thing to do. I should have been watching my back. The opposing Red fullback could not resist
this perfect target for a flying tackle and I was thrown to
the ground and landed on my head.

Over many decades, polo and rugby matches had hardened
the ground. I was unconscious for a few moments, just long
enough for my teammates to gather around. Their remarks
were unsettling: "You've killed him," and, "Maybe it's just
a broken neck," said with not a hint of regret.

I moved my arms and legs and neck and realized I had escaped damage. It was a great relief not to be dead. Spitting
grass and expletives I looked up at my father, who towered
above me. I was still a little dazed and his body seemed a

shield hung up between me and the afternoon sun. I was pulled to my feet and my father said, "Always watch your back." Then turning to my teammates he said, "I just heard a news broadcast from London. England has declared war on Germany." It was September 3rd, 1939.

Rugby Team, 1939. Sir George Roberts on right.

This ended our practice. My father returned to his news broadcasts. Some of us sought the shelter of a nearby silk-cotton tree. Its spreading branches formed a green canopy with a view of Hog Island across the harbour. Tombstones from centuries before, long neglected, provided seats and back rests.

No one spoke for a while and then someone said, "Well, I hope the Governor sends a telegram to England that we are right behind her."

"Yes," said another, "and aren't we lucky to be three thousand miles behind her."

I was silent, thinking of two older brothers who shared our father's condemnation of Hitler's belligerence. My brothers had sworn to "join up" if war was declared. But they were reluctant to say so in our father's presence. "What will happen now?" I thought, "Which service will they join?"

An inscription on a nearby tombstone reminded me that the pathway of life, whether as civilian or serviceman, inevitably leads to the wasteland of death. The carved lettering, weathered by sun and salt spray, was read with difficulty.

> Remember man as you pass by
> As you are now so once was I
> As I am now so you will be
> Remember man, eternity.

It was all too bewildering for our young minds to contemplate. We were teenagers, still wet around the ears, insular in our thinking but confident that the war would be over before we could volunteer for service. The mighty British Empire and our older brothers would soon get rid of Hitler.

It was much later when I understood that within me a primal excitement was already stirring. Exposed to the tales of Rudyard Kipling and George Alfred Henty and with the naïveté of youth, war to us meant high adventure in far places and a chance to escape the confines of our island.

On a more profound level there was an atavistic compulsion to defend the gates and repel the enemy. Our patriotism, though diluted by two centuries of colonial exile, could not be denied. Our Loyalist forefathers had sought a new life in the Bahamas in 1785, rather than sever their ties to England.

In the branches of a stately silk cotton tree the pigeons were settling in for the night. It was time to go. As I walked home the houses and gardens were in shadow. The eastern sky suddenly darkened but the western sky was still alive with thinning streaks of flame. And then the sun went down and the first stars appeared.

CHAPTER 2:

1941

Nassau

Two years before, when war was declared, my brothers Hartis and Leonard, bought Dad a new radio. It was an Atwater Kent, and the best available, a bulky contraption attached by cable to a large battery. The speakers were behind a fabric-covered aperture.

Dad kept us and the neighbours well informed. Hitler was on the rampage in Europe and Africa. Dad condemned him with colourful nautical invective. My younger brother, Maurice, and I were impressed and sometimes tried out the swear words on our older brother, Roscoe.

To our secret delight Roscoe would give chase. We were faster and usually got away. Sometimes he would chase us all the way to the Eastern Parade.

Our favourite expression, "you copper-bottomed son of a bitch," was especially annoying to Roscoe. In due course we shortened it to 'Old Copper Bottom,' but only used it if there was a clear way of escape.

Hitler's invasion of Poland on September 1st 1939 was followed by declarations of war on Germany by England and France. Astonishingly, thereafter, there was a prolonged period of inactivity, later described by former Prime Minister Chamberlain as "the twilight war."

On land and in the air the protagonists paused: Germany the aggressor, was poised to strike, England contented herself with dropping pamphlets over Germany and the French Army sat, mobilized but motionless, on the border with Germany.

In retrospect, it is clear that this lull was to England's advantage. Winston Churchill, member of the War Cabinet, and now Prime Minister led and inspired the various government departments. There was frantic improvement of England's defences and the British Army prepared to aid France on the continent.

Survivor of Athenia sinking, Sept. 3, 1939.

However, at sea there was action from the first day of war. At 9pm on September 3rd, the passenger liner *Athenia* was torpedoed by a German U-boat, with a loss of 112 lives, including 28 American citizens. On September 13th the British aircraft carrier *Courageous* was sunk close to home in the Bristol Channel. When, at 1:30am on October 14th, the battleship *Royal Oak* was torpedoed inside the defenses of Scapa Flow, on the North Scottish coast, Dad gave grudging admiration to the U-boat commander, Gunter Priem. Dad was echoing Winston Churchill who, as First Lord of the Admiralty, reported to Parliament, "This entry by a U-boat must be considered a remarkable exploit of professional skill and daring."

Before the end of October more than a dozen ships had been sunk, some at the entrance to English harbours. The U-boat War was on and would continue, with increasing activity, for three long years. At times more ships would be lost than could be replaced. England's fate would depend on winning what in due course would be called the Battle of the Atlantic.

CHAPTER 3

Late 1941

Nassau

We were sitting in the shade of the front porch of our house on Dowdeswell Street. The daily ice delivery truck came by and Mom bought a four-penny slab of ice for the icebox. The smell of fresh baked cinnamon rolls drifted across the road from Louis' Greek Bakery. If we timed it right Maurice and I could buy one of yesterdays rolls at half price (one penny), if we could borrow a penny.

"You can forget this nonsense about joining the British Navy," said my father. My brother Maurice and I were silent. Since our two older brothers had gone overseas, Hartis to the Royal Air force, and Leonard to the Royal Canadian Air force, Dad often made similar statements.

Born in 1885, Dad had spent a lifetime in sailing ships, with voyages throughout the Caribbean and along the East Coast of the United States. Now the retired captain of a three-master, and partially crippled from a leg injury, he spent his days listening to BBC broadcasts, railing at Adolph Hitler and worrying that two more sons would go away to the War.

Seeking to discourage us from joining the British Navy he was quite prepared to re-arrange history. He often spoke of the Navy's previous harsh disciplinary customs, as if they applied to the Royal Navy of the Twentieth Century.

Maurice and I referred to it as Dad's 'cat o' nine tails speech.'

My mother was more direct. "Outrageous lies," she said.

We never knew what imaginative distortions would be included. Now, on the front porch, he was in full stride; his voice rang out, loud and clear, from a lifetime of giving orders at sea. Passers-by stopped to listen. Someone shouted, "You tell 'em, cap'n, you tell 'em." We looked away. Mom retreated indoors.

"You know, they use the cat-o-nine tails for even minor infringements. You're tied to the mast and beaten with the 'cat,' a whip made of knotted leather, each of its nine tentacles tipped with brass or bone. When not in use it is kept in a red baize bag to conceal the blood. You're in serious trouble when they let the 'cat out of the bag.' Ten strokes and the flesh is flayed from the bones. And then you're thrown to the sharks."

Maurice and I looked at each other and then across to the bakery. Soon all of yesterday's rolls would be sold.

Dad continued, "You don't know what it's like to be keel-hauled, do you? You're tied to a rope and dragged along the ship's bottom, from one side to the other. Most sailors drown or are so scarred by barnacles they die soon after."

We refrained from asking how many keel-haulings he'd witnessed. He did not take kindly to sarcasm.

"And many sailors do not return from long voyages. Scurvy gets them and they're buried at sea. Those who survive are changed forever. They go blind, their teeth fall out and their private parts turn blue, shrivel up and fall off."

Dad had never been so graphic. Maurice and I looked at each other in alarm and shuddered involuntarily. My mother hurried on to the porch, "That's enough," she said to dad, "come inside, it's time for the war news."

She then handed us four pennies, "Get two fresh cinnamon rolls," she said. She could always read our thoughts.

My childhood friend, Annabel Lee, moved to England in 1937, with her family, when she was 16. Infrequent letters and Christmas cards told of her busy life at boarding school. I thought of her often, but seldom wrote.

In late December, I received a letter, posted almost two months earlier. I held the envelope and turned it over for several minutes, restraining an impulse to rip it open. Finally, I retreated to the back porch, away from street noises and interruptions. The envelope was creased and stained by its long journey. I opened it slowly and felt a surge of excitement as I spread the pages and saw the familiar handwriting.

October 12th, 1940

My dear Chester,

You've been a very naughty boy. Why haven't you written? Maybe you have written and the letters went astray, so consider yourself forgiven.

I hear from a friend in Abaco that you have volunteered for service in the Royal Navy. I am so excited at the thought of seeing you again, but must confess that I am quite confused, as I wonder if you really know what you're getting into.

Firstly, you have to survive the Atlantic crossing; many ships are being sunk by German U-boats. You will probably do your basic training at Royal Naval Barracks in Portsmouth, a target for German bombers. And then, when you finish basic training you never know where you'll be sent.

All this makes me a silly hypocrite as, since I last wrote, I joined the WRNS – Women's Royal Naval Service. I guess I'm lucky to be alive, as when we did basic training (we're told not to use place names), the Jerries came over almost every night. It was sheer hell and very chaotic. We practically lived in the shelters but that's no good if there's a direct hit. That's what happened, and some of my friends were killed.

I was lucky on that tragic night as I ignored the alarm at first and just had time to jump into a slit trench instead of going to the main shelter, which got a direct hit. I hugged the earth and prayed and was more frightened than I'd ever been in all my life and was deafened for days.

But enough of that and I'm now in a much safer place which will be nameless. The training is a piece of cake, and I have been recommended for a course which will, if all goes well, make me an officer, with one gold stripe on each sleeve. Will you be proud of me?

I often remember when we picked seagrapes at Tilloo Cay and that night at Hope Town when we played Big Ring. I can close my eyes and see the clear water and sandy beaches and the sunsets across the Sea of Abaco. If I'm very still and in a quiet place, I can actually hear the sound of the waves breaking on Camel's Reef and smell the scent of sea geranium from the shores of Pelican Cay and Lynyard Cay.

Do you remember that special day when we went turbot fishing? The sky was so blue and the sea so calm and clear that it seemed the dinghy was floating above the earth. I can still see the turbots fighting for my bait and feel the exciting tug on the hand-line when I hooked a big one.

I guess I'm homesick and if you come to England, you can tell me all about it as I know you love it so.

Please give my regards to your family and to Thomas Sweeting from Man-o-war Cay, as I hear he is also trying to join the Navy.

You have my parents' address, so please, please, write to me soon and let me know if and when you're coming.

Love and five kisses XXXXX,

Annabel

CHAPTER 4

Nassau

Eve of Departure

Sometime in December 1941 we were summoned by letter to a meeting with the Colonial Secretary. The official envelope was stamped "ON HIS MAJESTY'S SERVICE" and the enclosed letter was in the archaic form in use at the time. It began:

> 'Dear Sir,
> I beg to request your presence,'

and ended with,

> I am, sir,
> Your most obedient servant.'

The Secretariat was a two-storey building in downtown Nassau, flanked by the House of Parliament and the main Post Office, and guarded by a statue of Queen Victoria. The old Queen looked regally across a landscaped square to Nassau harbour – and beyond, to her island in the North Sea, now under siege by the tyrant Hitler.

The Secretary was responsible for governing the Colony but with increasing constraints imposed by an independent local Parliament. The Royal Governor, Edward, Duke of Windsor, and deposed King of England, played a mainly ceremonial role; with great reluctance, it was said.

After waiting in an outer room of the Secretariat we were finally ushered into the Secretary's office. There were only four chairs so we all stood. The Secretary unwound his long frame from his chair and stood facing us. He was tall and quite thin, with patchy red hair, and to our untrained eyes, seemed to have an air of distinction. He came from behind the desk and very solemnly shook our hands, as we murmured our names.

He then stood facing us, "Good morning gentlemen." We all stood a bit straighter. I thought, how appropriate, but farcical, to be labeled "gentlemen" by the person who, in his letter, referred to himself as "our obedient servant," but who was in fact the second highest official in the Bahamas.

He continued, "I have good news for you. The Treasury has approved funds necessary for your passage from Nassau to Halifax, Nova Scotia. As many convoys leave from that port it is expected that you will continue your journey to England by ship."

He scratched the top of his head and one of the red patches became a red tuft. "You will also be pleased to hear that the Treasury has granted to each of you the generous sum of ten pounds. You will need to buy warm clothing and there will, of course, be many expenses on your long journey." We were surprised and pleased. We had not requested financial help. It might have been my imagination but I thought a fleeting smile crossed the Secretary's face when he described ten pounds as a generous amount.

He explained that travel arrangements would be made by his office and we would be given details later. He then became less formal and told us that his father served in the Royal Navy in the Great War and that we were "plucky chaps" to volunteer for the "Senior Service."

It must have been evident that we were eager to leave and

share our news. With a final round of handshakes and a cordial "Cheerio chaps" from the Secretary, we were ushered out.

Mom and Dad were sitting on the front porch when Maurice and I returned from the Secretariat. We were nervous as we told them that our departure for England would be within a few weeks.

Dad was silent. Mom stood up quickly and went inside. We fidgeted and after what seemed a long time, Dad spoke. "I'm not surprised," he said. "And you'll get no more sermons from me. In any case," he continued, with a smile, "I was running out of fibs." Maurice and I looked at each other in relief.

He then did a surprising thing. With walking stick in left hand, he pushed himself upright, standing tall with straight back and squared shoulders. Maurice and I looked at each other and then, instinctively, stood at attention, facing him.

He looked directly at us and said, "My boys, I'm proud of you. If I was ten years younger and had two good legs I'd go with you; that evil bastard, Hitler, must be beaten."

He then saluted us, with right arm stiff, bent at the elbow, hand and fingers straight and held just above his right brow; the Royal Navy salute[1], indicating a sailor shading his eyes as he looks toward the horizon.

---

[1] It was not always thus. In the days of Lord Nelson there was a greater gulf between officers and other ranks. Sailors or those of lowly rank, on meeting their superiors, showed subservience by touching or pulling their forelocks accompanied by a slight bow. Presumably the modern salute evolved to preserve discipline, but without servility.

CHAPTER 5

A Royal Farewell

Our departure date was suddenly upon us. A note from the Colonial Secretary's office "begged to inform us" that all was arranged: departure from Nassau for Miami by Pan American seaplane and thence by train to New York and Halifax. We had just three weeks. Life became frantic.

At short notice we were summoned to a meeting with the Duke of Windsor at Government House. A faded photograph shows our group of twelve standing behind the seated Governor. Our clothes reveal de rigueur of the early forties: some of us in white trousers and black and white shoes. Sixty years later my granddaughters are amused and declare our apparel as "definitely uncool."

The Governor's residence, an impressive mansion, was built in 1801 on a high ridge overlooking the town and harbour. While of modest height the ridge is known boastfully as Mount Fitzwilliam, perhaps to flatter the then Royal Governor, Fitzwilliam. Purple and white bougainvillea flow over massive cut-stone boundary walls, from which a statue of Christopher Columbus gazes seaward, to the ocean on which he made his heroic voyages and changed the course of history forever.

On arriving at Government House we were shown to a waiting room. Soon our entire group had assembled. While waiting we discussed the extensive renovations to Government House, made in 1940, to accommodate the Duke of

Windsor and his new wife. The town gossips maintained that the Duchess was not impressed, complained bitterly of the heat and was contemptuous of Bahamians. While devoted to her Edward, she made frequent trips to the United States to get away from a place that, by later admission, she hated.

Ever the romantic, my brother Maurice said, "Forget those catty town gossips. You have to admit that it is the love story of the ages. The King of England, Emperor of India, Head of the Commonwealth gave it all up to be with the woman he loved. You should be sorry for him if she turned out to be a spoiled brat." The entrance of the Governor's aide-de-camp ended further discussion.

The aide conducted us to a terrace overlooking a landscaped area, with inviting pathways and statuary. The Governor in a white linen suit was seated. A photographer placed us so that we stood behind His Excellency. We arranged our faces into our individual perception of the "meeting with royalty" look. For most of us this was a blank stare; for others, the slightly pained look from too tight underwear.

Volunteers for Royal Navy with Duke of Windsor, 1942.

While seated, His Royal Highness, in a white linen suit, appeared quite regal; an effect lost when he stood, because of his diminutive height. He was gracious, shook our hands and murmured encouraging remarks about our coming journey.

It was over very quickly and we were ushered out. I had missed my chance to make small talk with the former King of England, Emperor of India and Head of the Commonwealth. Perhaps, just as well, I might have offered to look up his brother, George VI, now the successor of all these titles.

Sadly, later years confirmed that behind the media-inspired, sympathetic, Edward, Prince of Wales, there was a selfish, naïve and shamefully disloyal individual. He deserted his family and his countrymen, particularly the lower classes he pretended to champion. By the thousands they chose to defend and die for England while Edward and Wallis played footsies with Hitler and Ribbentrop.

The House of Windsor was redeemed by Edward's younger brother, George, who took on the role of Monarch, performed his ceremonial duties with distinction, and earned respect from the free world.

CHAPTER 6

On Our Way

Our flight from Nassau would be the beginning of a journey into unknown territory. Where our journey would end we knew not but it was exciting to ponder the fateful pathways ahead.

I had flown just once before. My brother Leonard, then a student pilot, took me up in a two-man training plane. It was a clear cloudless day. I was enjoying the birds-eye view of Hog Island and the toy houses and boats far below, when I foolishly asked, "How do you get out of a spin?"

Without replying, Leonard pulled the nose up until the plane stalled. When the nose dropped away the resulting spin seemed to go on forever, the boats and houses became larger, the earth rushed up to meet us and then, suddenly, we were once again flying straight and level, but just above the treetops. I was scared out of my wits and none the wiser about how to get out of a spin. My main concern was getting out of the plane.

I had no fears about flying on the Commodore, a Pan American seaplane. Flight time to Miami would be two hours, at an altitude of 800 feet, unless delayed by head winds.

Family and friends of our group were at the Pan American Terminal, near the Eastern Parade, to bid farewell. There were some tears but mostly a forced cheerfulness as we lined up on the ramp to board the plane.

I took a last look across the road to the Eastern Parade, scene of innumerable rugby matches. St. Matthew's church was partially hidden by surrounding ancient trees, which matched the church in age.

Giant almond trees along the border of the parade were shedding leaves, the ground beneath carpeted in gold and brown leaves. In the old cemetery nearby hibiscus bloomed between the gravestones.

Maurice and I embraced Mom and Dad briefly. We had said our family goodbyes at home. When I hugged brother Roscoe he whispered, "Always remember, the sharp end is the bow and the blunt end is the stern."

I said, "Thanks for your advice Old Copper Bottom." I think there were tears in his eyes. I know there were in mine.

As we taxied onto Montagu Bay there was just a whisper of wind from the east. With a full load and lack of wind we ran for a long time at full throttle. The sea was reluctant to let us go. Nassau shrank to a blur on the horizon. Someone said, "Exuma here we come." Finally, the sea released us to the sky. Very slowly we gained sufficient altitude and banked on to the course for Miami.

I was in a window seat. Fate had arranged a perfect Bahamian day for our departure: a few fluffy white clouds to accentuate the lapis lazuli blue of the sky and, just below, a sea so calm and clear that every reef was outlined; occasional sharks and stingrays could be seen. The marls and creeks of Andros, evidence of its unhurried emergence from the sea, marched to the south and disappeared into the misty distance; a blue and green void, shrouding a destiny toward which we now hastened.

Suddenly the panorama of crystal-clear shallow seas changed to a dark blue. We were now flying over the mile deep Gulf Stream. Soon a blur on the horizon became the coast of Florida and the buildings of Miami appeared in the distance.

Miami of the early forties was just a decade or two from its beginnings as a village at the mouth of the Indian River. My older brothers remembered being there as boys with my father on the Alma R, a three mast sailing ship. They moored to a dock, which jutted through mangroves on the south side of the river. Now in 1942, the downtown development was limited to a small area on the North side of the river mouth.

There was no time for sightseeing. We were taken from the plane to a railroad station and boarded a train for the overnight journey to New York.

Our three-day stay in New York was the first manifestation of a serendipity that seemed to follow me on my journeys. Fate often made me the beneficiary of chance happenings. I would meet people of ability and passion who became friends and helped me on my way. My brother Maurice put it simply: "You're the luckiest man I know," he said.

We planned that on arrival in New York we would seek the cheapest accommodation available for our three-day stay. Our expectations were not high.

Before leaving Nassau I had written Max Feinberg, a family friend, with homes in New York and Nassau. I told him of our short visit and suggested a brief meeting.

When we arrived at Union Station, tired from our long journey, Max appeared and explained that he had arranged accommodation for all of us at the Barbizon Plaza Hotel. He also had plans for our entertainment. We were astonished and grateful for his generosity.

Max was a homely man, short with a roly-poly stomach. Wispy grey hair framed an earnest face. Without notice, he often burst into Polish or Russian folk songs, sometimes so sentimental that his eyes would fill with tears. To make us laugh he sang a risqué song about a naughty little flea looking for a hiding place.

We learned later that some of Max's family in Europe were victims of Hitler's genocide. Max's generosity to our group, volunteers in the fight against Hitler, was a gesture of gratitude and solidarity.

With Max as our guide the three days passed quickly. The city was a wonderland to most of us. We ate at the Automat, rode on the subways and joined other tourists on neck stretching looks at the skyscrapers.

For our first evening, Max arranged good seats at Radio City Music Hall. We were wide-eyed when the Rockettes came on stage and marveled at their famous routines of precision dancing and shoulder high kicks. Being lusty young men, our equanimity was strained by the near nudity and bounteous bosoms.

On our last day Max arranged a trip to Coney Island and its Carnival attractions. The day is memorable for an incident on the subway to Coney Island. It was a sharp reminder that I was now in a different world. My life in Abaco and Nassau had been one of small town neighbourliness: caring for others, kindliness and common courtesy. These were rules for living that most people followed. On this day I would realize that in larger communities it is necessary to be on guard against malice. In these circumstances common courtesy is often uncommon.

As the train made its way to Coney Island I was seated near the sliding entrance doors. When the door slid open at the various stations there would be a temporary congestion of arriving and departing passengers.

At one station an attractive young lady jumped on, moments before the doors slid shut. As she did so a bracelet from her wrist fell onto the platform. She was apparently unaware of her loss. In a flash I left my seat, jumped onto the platform, retrieved the bracelet and turned quickly to beat the closing doors. I didn't quite make it. As the door slid shut the rubber flanges on each side came neatly to rest on my neck.

My head was inside the compartment; a Clown, looking wide-eyed, open mouth and stupid at the grinning passengers. My body from the neck down was dangling outside, my black and white shoes beating a tattoo on the platform.

My entrapment was just for a few seconds. An alert conductor pressed a button, the door opened and I jumped into the train, clutching the retrieved bracelet.

I then abandoned my role of Clown and became Sir Galahad, riding to the aid of a lady. The bracelet owner was sitting. As befits a knight I made a slight bow and offered her the bracelet.

She felt her wrist to confirm that her bracelet was missing, jumped to her feet, slapped me on the face, grabbed the bracelet and shouted, "You f-----g thief. I'll call the police." I retreated to the far end of the compartment.

Our afternoon at Coney Island passed quickly. Our favourite ride was a roller coaster, aptly called "The Cyclone Chaser." After that, the Ferris wheel seemed quite tame, even though brother Maurice and I were left dangling upside-down in a malfunctioning chair, at the top of the wheel, while other passengers were taken on below. Not trusting the restraining straps, we desperately clutched the seat while coins from our clothing rained to the ground to be quickly pocketed.

I had my fortune told by The Great Zelda, a lady of voluminous proportions. She was well named. Even though she was seated in an oversized chair, portions of Zelda spilled over the arms.

I sat in a chair opposite while she gazed into her crystal ball. Inky black eyes were framed by eyelashes dripping with mascara. Acres of bosom rested on the table, displaying a miniature Grand Canyon of cleavage. Her impenetrable black eyes had noted my shoes and my suntan. Her massive face twitched when she heard my Bahamian accent.

When she looked up from her crystal ball and spoke, it was in a throaty but quite pleasant voice. But first she looked around and lowered her voice, as if not to be overheard while imparting profound secrets. She said that I was on a journey, that I lived in the south in a hot climate where one often did not wear shoes. I was in love with a beautiful girl and would be receiving a letter; and that the reading would cost two dollars. For another two dollars she was prepared to look deeper into the crystal ball.

I thanked Zelda for her offer, paid two dollars and walked away. Her charming flim-flam was worth the price. For another two dollars I might have learned that my mother loved me and that I would be receiving a telegram.

CHAPTER 7

Halifax to London

My memory of the journey from New York to Halifax is limited to images of vast forests, through which the train ran interminably. At night, with my companions sprawled asleep, I sat with my face against the cold glass of the window. As the train, with monotonous clickety-clack and mournful whistle, hurtled northward, firefly flashes of light indicated human habitation in the wilderness.

There were long hours to ponder why I was on this train in the dark night, stretching the umbilical cord of my being ever further from home. I could be lying on a warm Bahamian beach but had chosen to take part in a war. Was I motivated by patriotism, escaping the confines of island life or testing my manhood? Or a combination of all of these? I was comforted by the words of Shakespeare:

> What is a man
> If his chief good and market of his time
> Be but to sleep and feed? A beast, no more.
> Sure, he that made us with such large discourse
> Looking before and after, gave us not
> That capability and god-like reason
> To fust in us unused.

Presumably, we traversed portions of New York state, Connecticut, Massachusetts, New Hampshire, Maine, New Brunswick and finally into Nova Scotia and south to Halifax. Halifax was founded in 1749 as a naval and military base, because of its geographic location and magnificent harbour. The indigenous Mik Maq Indians called the area Chebucto – or biggest harbour.

Halifax is a wonderful example of the truism, "people make the place." Resolve and courage has marked all its generations. In December 1917, when an ammunition ship collided with another ship, the city suffered the largest man-made explosion, before the nuclear age. Thousands were killed and injured and most of the city destroyed.

Twenty-five years later in 1942, when we arrived, most of the wounds had healed and Halifax was a strategic mobilization and transshipment point. Supply convoys from its harbour would save Britain from defeat.

While awaiting passage to Britain we were accommodated at the Canadian Naval Barracks at Dartmouth, across the harbour from Halifax. Our status could best be described as working guests.

We were still civilians. To pay for our keep we became part of the work force. Kitchen detail and latrine detail were our most frequent jobs. We must have been good at it. Six weeks passed before passage to England was arranged.

There may have been another reason for the delay. We were impatient to be gone and resisted suggestions by the Naval officer in command that we join the Canadian Navy. Some of our group were of the opinion that earlier passage was delayed, hoping that our minds could be changed. Time has blurred the details but we became quite aggrieved. Fortunately, before it became an open issue we were informed that departure would be in three days.

It turned out that delay had worked to our advantage, fulfilling Uncle Whittleton's adage that "there is an advantage in every disadvantage." We were given passage on the *SS Batory*, a prewar Polish luxury liner. Now used as a troop ship, the *Batory* would sail in company with another troop ship, both capable of sustaining speeds of 18 knots[2]. When both ships cleared the submarine nets, deployed at the harbour entrance, we were joined by two escorts that took stations on the port and starboard bows.

SS Batory - ex-Polish luxury liner.

Fast moving and hopefully able to elude the U-boats, we set off at 18 knots. Slower and larger convoys suffered heavy losses, committed as they were to the speed of the slowest ship, often only 7 knots. In April and May 185 ships were sunk and in June losses would be 173 ships (834,196 tons).

On only one occasion did we change from an easterly course. At about midpoint in the voyage , early one morning, we were awakened by a change of motion and a surge upward in the throb of the engines. At daylight we made our way on deck. Our sister troop ship was almost hull down to the west, one escort could be seen far ahead, with the other hull down to the east. For the rest of the day we charged northward but sometime during the night resumed our easterly course.

---

[2] About 20.73 miles per hour

We learned later that our change of course was in response to an intelligence report that a U-boat patrol line had been detected a hundred miles directly ahead; at our speed just a five-hour run to harms way.

With our superior speed we could outrun U-boats astern or on our flank; only a coordinated attack by an enemy, lying in wait, had any chance of success. This was foiled by our end run around the U-boat pack.

Memory retains few details of the passage. There were several hundred troops, some of whom passed the time in marathon poker sessions. We had no money for gambling but enjoyed watching. The weather was good and when not watching poker games we spent the daylight hours in some sheltered area of the top deck.

We were on deck early on the seventh day having been told that land would be sighted sometime during the morning. Securing a place near the bow we looked eagerly ahead. The rising sun illuminated the eastern horizon and soon a speck, fine on the port bow, took on substance. It was Goat Fell, a 2800 feet peak on the Isle of Arran, which straddles the approaches to the Clyde Estuary. Very quickly other land appeared; the coast of Ayrshire off to starboard and the lovely undulating hills of Arran to port.

As we went further into the Firth of Clyde, shafts of sun-light touched the tops of purple hills. Mist in the valleys, infused with soft light, drifted upward in tenuous strands and disappeared. We were soon near enough to see sheep grazing and streams coursing down the hillsides. For some reason tears welled up in my eyes. Perhaps some mystical connection to the departure of my forefathers from these shores, three centuries earlier. Or maybe, just the pure joy of gazing at a landscape so beautiful that tears are in-voked.

Soon all our group were on deck, excited and smiling at the

end of this stage of our journey. It had been an easy crossing. The often cruel North Atlantic had shown an unusually kind face and we had eluded a deadly "wolf pack" of U-boats.

The great anchorage at the mouth of the Clyde was filled with hundreds of ships, of all types and sizes: passenger liners, merchant ships, escorts, coasting vessels, all anchored, seemingly in great confusion. The *Batory* made her way cautiously down a lane at the side of the anchorage and into Greenock.

Hemmed in by hills, Greenock stretched along a cramped waterside. The limited space was also a base for the Free French Navy. A residential area on the heights overlooked a waterside industrial location. Somehow, in this congestion, the *Batory* found dock space to disembark hundreds of troops.

Our group did not disembark until the next day. Extra time was needed to find the Resident Naval Officer and arrange our journey south. Like errant school children we set off in single file, through the narrow crowded street, along the waterfront. Some two miles away after frequently asking directions, we finally found the right address. We were dealt with by an irritable Petty Officer, puzzled by our accents and not sure where we should be sent.

Someone in our group remembered a copy of a letter from the Colonial Secretary in Nassau, directed to an individual in Rex House in London. This was produced, to the great relief of the Petty Officer, who quickly produced Railway passes from Glasgow to London.

Retrieving our luggage from the *Batory* we made our way to Glasgow Railway Station. Two compartments were secured by fleet-of-foot brother Maurice and cousin Alan Russell and we settled in for the ten hour journey to London. Most of our fellow passengers were in uniform, a reminder that we were now on an island under siege.

On arrival in London we made our way to the Overseas League. Located on the Strand in Central London this organization had been formed to help servicemen from the Colonies. The kind ladies of the League, all volunteers, were unfazed by the unannounced arrival of twelve Bahamians, with luggage, and soon arranged accommodation in various nearby hotels and hostelries.

We decided, unanimously, that a pause in our journey was in order and, for this, there was no better place than London, even at the risk of a German bombing raid. After a few days we could make a final leap into our destinies.

My impressions of London had been formed by the writings of Charles Dickens, Conan Doyle, George Bernard Shaw and a host of authors and poets reaching back to Geoffrey Chaucer. They had not led me astray but now, walking its streets, I discovered another multi-layered London; one that was far more than a collection of meandering streets and old buildings. A city with a soul, a life force, that seemingly gained strength from disaster: its razing by Boadicea in 61AD, the Great Fire of 1666 which destroyed 13,000 buildings and the Great Plague which killed over one hundred thousand.

The recent German bombing for fifty-seven consecutive nights exposed the unconquerable heart's core of London. Inexplicably, standing in the rubble of a devastated square mile, I felt only defiance emanating from the ashes. My commitment to serve in the Navy was reaffirmed.

Many of London's sights were manageable by foot. Often it was more convenient to divide into subgroups, according to our individual interests. Sometimes it was preferable to explore alone.

We visited St. Paul's Cathedral, the Christopher Wren

masterpiece; a symbol of survival, as German bombs had devastated many nearby buildings. Our tour included Big Ben, The Houses of Parliament, Westminster Abbey and Buckingham Palace; all famous landmarks. We were intrigued by the Bahama ducks in the wild bird sanctuary at St. James Park.

Trafalgar Square, nearest to our accommodations, was the most popular destination. Nelson's Column with the famous bronze lions was often our rendezvous. One day I was too late to join our group. They had gone to chat up girls who often ate their lunch in St. James Park. Feeling somewhat left out, I ventured into St. Martins-in-the-Field Church and, soothed by its simplicity, sat for a while. A contrast to its otherwise simple interior was the rich Italian plasterwork on the barrel vault ceiling.

A pleasant surprise, as I sat, was the performance of a free lunchtime concert. There were few people in the church but excerpts from Mozart and Grieg were played with an enthusiasm and concentration in keeping with a packed concert hall. Exquisite harmonies filled the Church and swirled upward to the ceiling, so that for a brief time we were soaring in a peaceful realm, far above war and destruction.

On the lighter side we walked one evening into Leicester Square and Piccadilly Circus, an exploration limited by the blackout and our lack of money for bars and nightclubs. Our numbers provided safety from the Piccadilly ladies-of-the-night. However, like wolves stalking a herd of deer, a bold couple managed to separate Maurice and Alan from our group. The rest of us stood nearby and listened to the exchange.

"Can we take you two handsome gentlemens to our flat and show you a good time?" was mischievously answered by Maurice with, "Are you inviting us to dinner?"

The girls flounced off, muttering scornfully, "Didn't your muvvers ever tell you nuffink?" Maurice shouted after them, "Thanks for asking anyway, but we've already had dinner!"

We all agreed that the time had now come for the next stage of our adventures. On our fourth morning we descended on Rex House in St. James Street. The usual bewilderment ensued. They didn't know who we were or whether we were coming or going. Producing our now well worn copy of the letter from the Colonial Secretary we found ourselves sitting in front of Commander Hartford, the officer to whom the letter was addressed. He said that the original had not been received.

Commander Hartford, tall and thin, with a casual manner, seemed kindly disposed but not at all eager to get to the point. He reminisced at length about his visits to Nassau on a warship in peacetime. I decided that he was buying time while he considered various options for dealing with us.

Finally, he said, "Why would you leave that lovely warm climate and come to this cold northern one?" No one responded. Then he ventured, "So what do you want to do?"

My brother Maurice, giving me a wink, said, "We want to be officers."

This got the Commander's attention. He threw his hands up, palms outward, as if we had asked for the Holy Grail. "Oh no, no, it doesn't work quite like that," he said.

He excused himself and in a few minutes returned. "I've got you sorted out," he said. "I've been in touch with

Training Commander Reid at Royal Naval Barracks, Portsmouth. You'll be going there for basic training. At the end of three months, you'll be sent to various ships as Ordinary Seamen."

He summoned a Petty Officer and gave instructions to issue railway warrants to Portsmouth. Commander Hartford then cordially shook hands all around and wished us good luck. Maurice was last in line. The Commander shook his hand, gave him a friendly tap on the shoulder and said, "Goodbye, Admiral!"

Ordinary Seaman, Chester Thompson, 1942.

CHAPTER 8

Of Bombs and Bluebells

On arrival in Portsmouth we were sent across the harbour to Gosport for the first four weeks of training. There we met our Instructor, Petty Officer Pattendon, an unforgettable character, with a split personality. On the parade ground he was a feared tyrant, a master of naval invective; loud mouthed and sarcastic he could intimidate the boldest rating.

If someone mixed up left and right he would roar, "You imbecile. I'll have your guts for garters; now five times around the parade ground, at the double."

Off the parade ground he was a gentle soul and on short acquaintance would invite ratings to his home in Southsea, already crowded with wife and five children.

We were now attired in blue bell-bottomed trousers, blue pullover jacket with three white stripes on a deep collar that covered the shoulders and a white dickey front with a blue banded top. Black hobnailed boots and a round sailor hat completed the uniform.

For four weeks we endured "square bashing," the naval term for marching interminably up and down a concrete square and running laps around its perimeter. In a short time the nails on the shoe soles were worn smooth, allowing us to run and then leap into a fast sliding motion. If the surface was smooth concrete we could slide swiftly for several yards. This was useful for getting first in line at mealtimes.

When dismissed on the Parade ground the more athletic of our group usually got to the mess-deck first, to secure places for the slower ones. Favouritism, and in our case nepotism, inevitably resulted in larger helpings for one's mates.

The first to arrive were also allowed to dish out the food from containers already in place. This allowed us to have first go at "the gash," the naval term for leftovers. We were always hungry and seldom was any "gash" returned to the galley.

The Portsmouth area, an important naval centre, was a prime target for German bombers. The first attack after our arrival in Gosport came as a surprise.

Tommy Sweeting and I were given an evening's liberty. Some older hands recommended a pub about a mile from barracks. Once there we were befriended by Billy, a fat man in his forties with lots of hair and a foul mouth.

He bought us pints. "Cheers, Yanks," he said. "So what part of the f-----g States are you from?"

Tommy tried to explain, "We're not from the States, we're from the Bahamas."

"Oh yeah," said Billy, "I suppose you know the f-----g Duke of Windsor."

"Yes," said Tommy. "We had tea with him before leaving the Bahamas."

Billy turned to me, "Stop taking the piss outa me. I have a

brother in New York, I know a Yank when I hear one."

I gave up. "We're sorry Billy," I said, "We're Yanks from Peoria, Illinois." He was satisfied, leaned across the table and shook our hands. "I like Yanks," he said. "Thank you for joining our Navy. Just keep your f-----g hands off our women."

Several pints later, closing time was called. Billy bade us a fond, foul mouthed, goodbye and we set off for barracks.

When the Air raid warning siren sounded we decided to run to a shelter within the barracks. Driven by the ominous drone of German bombers and nearby explosions, we set off down the street at a good lick. Any Dutch courage from the beer vanished. In a second we were cold sober and scared. For some reason, fright made me think in Bahamian dialect. Perhaps, subconsciously, I wished desperately to be back home with familiar sights and sounds (Freud was a genius).

"Feets don't let us down!" I shouted to Tommy. Explosions coming nearer released a new wave of energy and I prayed aloud, "Lord, you pick up our feets, we'll put 'em down."

The barracks was further than we thought. We never made it. Somewhere just ahead a bomb exploded. A nearby antiaircraft battery was firing at the bombers. The combined noise was deafening and frightening.

There was no one else on the street. Flames erupted from a nearby building. We clambered over a gate and huddled in a doorway. Our frantic knocks went unanswered. The occupants were not dummies, they were in a shelter. The bombs continued to explode. We were both panting from our frantic run. Tommy seemed unruffled, "We never had this on Man-o-war Cay," he said.

An air raid warden appeared out of the noise and confusion. "You bloody fools!" he shouted, "Why aren't you in an air raid shelter?" He then directed us to a shelter a short distance back. We had passed it on our headlong flight.

We dove down a steep stairway and into the shelter. Several flashlights - sorry, torches - revealed a long underground space with seats on both sides. Everyone was calm. Mothers huddled at the far end, clutching babes in arms and young children.

We had interrupted a sing-a-long. It now continued with a bawdy song of many verses about an amorous sailor and a willing lass. That finished, they looked at Tommy and me. Tommy pushed me to my feet.

I thought that after the naughty goings-on in the song it would be elevating to sing a good Methodist hymn. With bombs raining down I chose what seemed most appropriate: "Nearer my God to Thee, nearer to Thee."

This was greeted with, "Sit down sailor, we'd rather listen to the bombs."

The sounds of bombing now seemed further away. We assumed that Portsmouth across the harbour was being targeted. After what seemed a long time the all-clear sounded. We made our way to the barracks through ruined streets, finding our way around fire fighting and rescue crews, dealing with the aftermath. To our great relief the barracks had escaped a direct hit.

We were saddened to hear that amongst those killed was the brave Air Raid Warden who had directed us to the shelter. He had continued looking for other "bloody fools" and failed to take shelter himself.

Sometime, during the first week we were sent across the harbour to Portsmouth for a meeting with Training Commander Reid. He too had visited Nassau in peacetime, as an officer on a British warship. Referred to as "showing the flag" it was a way of reminding the colonies of England's protection and, no doubt, sending a message of England's might to any would-be foes.

Like Commander Hartford, at Rex House in London, Commander Reid had obviously enjoyed himself in Nassau. He spoke of dances in Nassau arranged by the then active IODE (International Order of the Daughters of the Empire). His tone was so wistful that I conjured up visions of pretty girls and handsome uniformed officers with kisses being exchanged under a Bahamian moon.

He soon became serious and reminded us that firstly we were there to be trained as Ordinary Seamen and that he expected us to do our best, before being sent to sea on one of His Majesty's ships.

He said that he was pleased to see in our resumés that some of us were rugby players. We would be called upon to play in the Portsmouth Barracks Team, recently defeated by "a bunch of thugs" sent by the RAF.

Captain Reid explained that if any of our group showed O.L.Q (officer like qualities) a file would be started on that individual. Known as a C.W. file (Commission Warranted) it would contain comments from the Training Staff, with final approval or rejection by the Training Commander. If approved, the individual while carrying out the duties of an Ordinary Seaman would also have the status of Cadet Rating.

The C.W. file would accompany the Cadet Rating when appointed to a ship. Should the Commanding Officer of the ship agree with the initial assessment (but only after a minimum of three months sea time) the Cadet could be sent ashore to be examined by a special Admiralty appointed Selection Board. Otherwise, at the discretion of the ship's

Commanding Officer additional sea time could be imposed or the C.W. file cancelled.

At the end of the fourth week we were given a long weekend of liberty – Friday morning to Tuesday evening. Brother Maurice and I traveled to Ely in Cambridgeshire to be the guests of a farmer, Hugh Markham, and his wife Grace. They were friends of Ernest Fleming, an Englishman we had known in the Bahamas, who arranged the invitation.

Mr. Markham met the train at Ely station and drove us to Fordy Farm. Their two-storied house with nearby barns and various farm buildings was in the middle of large acreage. The main crops were sugar beet and potatoes, vital commodities in wartime England. Pigs and chickens were kept, ensuring a supply of bacon and eggs. An extensive fruit orchard produced apples and plums in season.

Meeting the Markhams was the beginning of a wonderful friendship. It seemed that a happy chance, a serendipity, had led us to Fordy Farm. They were childless and before the weekend was over we had been adopted. At their request, they became Auntie Grace and Uncle Hugh. They seemed determined to spoil us and we put up little resistance.

Uncle Hugh was the quintessential gentleman farmer and would doff his cap with equal courtesy, whether meeting lady or milkmaid. Auntie, gentle and unpretentious, was loved in the area for her generosity and support of deserving causes.

We enjoyed walking with uncle as he supervised various activities. The acreage was part of a vast area of former marshland, transformed over three centuries, by systematic drainage, into flat arable land. The walks covered a wide area and resulted in keen appetites, to enjoy abundant meals, provided by Mrs. Slack, the genial cook-house-keeper.

One afternoon Maurice and I set off on our own. We crossed several fields and, on approaching a small wood, came across a crew of Women's Land Army, employed by Uncle. To our surprise we were greeted with whistles. As we approached they dropped their hoes. There were four of them, all tanned and fit. It was a warm day and they had discarded their green blouses and dungarees for open neck shirts and short skirts. This scant clothing revealed stunning feminine curves.

We stopped in our tracks. Maurice whispered, "We're outnumbered, let's surrender peacefully."

The girls were grateful to have a break from work and insisted on giving us tea from a blackened pot. We could not refuse.

We sat in a circle, in such close proximity that other hidden charms were revealed. We were soon in animated conversation. They were curious about our unfamiliar accents and we, in turn, wanted to know where they were from. Kitty from Cornwall had a degree in botany; Virginia was the daughter of a Lancashire miner; and the other two from Mold, a small Welsh village. They all loved the countryside and preferred working on the land to service in Army or Navy.

Kitty said, looking directly at Maurice, that there was a thick carpet of bluebells in the nearby woods. To my amusement Maurice said that bluebells were his favourite flower and that he must see them. As they disappeared I remembered that Auntie was expecting us for tea.

Retrieving my brother took some time and we ran the last half-mile. Auntie introduced us to the minister of a nearby church, his wife and some other local dignitaries.

I noticed during tea that Maurice's mind seemed to be elsewhere. He revealed where, when he said to me in an undertone, "I think I'm in love with Kitty."

I said, "So, did you enjoy seeing bluebells, your favourite flowers?"

He looked a bit puzzled, "What are bluebells?" he asked.

On returning from our weekend leave we were stationed at Portsmouth Barracks for the remaining eight weeks. "Square bashing" continued but there was also instruction in seamanship, signaling, self defence, etc.

Most of our group had sea-faring ancestors and, not surprisingly, did well on the sea oriented subjects. Rope splicing, especially splicing of wire rope, was tiresome but knot tying instruction seemed more suitable for boys of twelve. We had been weaned on half hitches and clove hitches. Bowlines, bowlines in the bight, sheet bends, sheepshanks and figures of eight were all familiar.

Our signaling Instructor, passionate about his subject, started out with pre-historic man beating on resonant logs with sticks and made his way to the last century, with the lighting of fires on line of sight hills. As recently as October 21st 1805, news of the victory of Lord Nelson at Trafalgar was transmitted from the South coast of England to London by hilltop beacons. Presumably news of Nelson's death came by mounted courier.

Just thirty-three years later, in 1838, Samuel Morse developed the Morse code, for the alphabet and numbers one to ten. Mainly used in wireless telegraphy its dash dot combinations were adapted for line of sight signaling lamps. The Aldis signaling lamp was widely used in the Royal Navy in World War II.

Our Instructor had us practice for hours with the Aldis lamp; partners at opposite ends of the Parade ground. If the Instructor was not present one was likely to receive quite crude messages. "FU2" was often the appropriate response.

Semaphore or visual signaling by means of flags, was widely used in World War II, particularly on small ships which often did not have radio or telegraphic equipment. It is accomplished by men who hold a small flag in each hand and, with arms extended, move them to different angles to indicate letters of the alphabet. Signalmen often become very skilful and the rapid movement of their flags can only be read by an equally skilful signalman.

"Stoney" Brown, our instructor in self defense was a cockney, who entertained us with colourful descriptions of various attack and defense positions. Most positions involved using the sharp rim of a steel helmet and hitting "Jerry" either on the throat or, preferably, in the "orchestra stalls" assuming you could get near enough.

We were puzzled. While aware of the vulnerability of "orchestra stalls" we knew that steel helmets were not issued equipment. "Stoney" was in his late forties and had been a soldier in World War I. I suspected that his teaching manual was also of World War I vintage.

Tests in the various subjects would be given at the end of the course and the results noted in our files. Also noted would be our proficiency in drilling and sports, as well as assessments by the training staff and, most importantly, by Training Commander Reid.

As promised by Commander Reid, the rugby players amongst our group became members of the Portsmouth Barracks Rugby team. Most of us had played since our early teens and, for some, this experience was backed up by special talents: David Lightbourn, quick on his feet, was remarkably deceptive in changing direction; my brother Maurice excelled at broken field running, changing angles without losing speed; Thomas Sweeting, fearless forward and aggressive attacker, also played well as a winger.

For weeks we practised for an upcoming contest with the RAF. To do so we were excused from "square bashing" and menial galley and cleaning details. If short of numbers we practised with teams of ten.

The big game was played on a Sunday afternoon on our home pitch, just outside Portsmouth. We were there as two buses drew up and the RAF team erupted on to the field. Commander Reid was right, some of the team looked decidedly "thuggish," perhaps intentionally; two hundred and forty pounders with no necks and manic expressions. It was evident there had been a pub stop or two – on the way from the RAF base.

They had only fourteen players, the fifteenth lost on the way, perhaps sleeping under a table at the last pub. To his great distress Tommy Sweeting was chosen to make up their fifteen.

Many of our supporters from the Barracks and town were there; Commander Reid and members of the training staff amongst them. The Commander was in civilian clothes and, throughout play, supported us with gusto, running along the sideline like a teenager.

The first half was a balls-up. The RAF forwards were sluggish, still feeling the effects of their pub crawl. Our forwards usually managed to get the ball out to the wings and two touchdowns were made, one by Maurice and the other by David. Both were converted, so that by half time the score was 10-0 in Navy's favour. Tommy Sweeting played valiantly as wing three-quarter for the RAF but the ball never got to him for a touch down attempt.

The second half was a different story. The RAF had sobered up and were determined to overwhelm us. The referee's whistle sounded often to break up ferocious clashes. Bodies would be revealed, strewn around as on a battlefield. Remarkably, there were no serious injuries and play continued.

We were busy defending our goal posts and unable to make another touch down. Several penalty kicks were attempted but all failed.

The RAF seemed to be getting stronger and scored two touchdowns and one conversion. The score stood at Navy 10 – RAF 8 when mercifully the referee blew the final whistle.

Our joyous supporters ran onto the field and carried Maurice and David around on their shoulders. Commander Reid was ecstatic, shook hands all around and said to the four of us, "Well done, Bahamas. Thank you."

The civilized traditional lineup for handshaking with our opponents was observed. The blows and bruises of the battlefield were forgotten and we united in camaraderie, until the next contest. Our recent foes on the field had just one concern: to which pub would we go for the usual postgame "pissup?"

CHAPTER 9

HMS Menestheus -- Minelayer

W e were nervous as we awaited posting to a ship. Somewhere in the Admiralty there was an office in which our futures were being decided. Fate was running a lottery. Our names were in a hat; the hand of Fate would hover, hesitate, and then pluck a name for service in a battleship, cruiser, destroyer, etc., on duty in the Atlantic, Mediterranean, the Far East, or elsewhere.

We all preferred service in smaller ships. On bigger ships one was anonymous. On the largest vessels the ships company might number two thousand or more. On smaller ships there was more camaraderie, less discipline, more opportunity for a motivated individual to excel.

The most desired posting was to a MTB, a Motor Torpedo Boat, with a crew of about a dozen. The excitement of night raids at a speed of 40-knots against larger enemy craft overshadowed the fragility of the vessels and high casualty rates.

My posting finally came through. It was not to a glamorous motor torpedo boat. Instead, I was ordered to report to *HMS Menestheus*, a minelayer, based in Kyle of Loch Alsh on the Northwest corner of Scotland. I was disappointed and shocked. Minelaying seemed boring and minelayers were, no doubt, slow and plodding. I would have to do something about it, but what?

I'd call Prime Minister Churchill, that's what I'd do. I then

had a better idea. I'd call King George. I had a great opening line: I would convey best regards from his older brother, Edward, and darling sister-in-law, Wallis, in Bahamas.
I would remind the King that my forebears were Loyalists
who stuck up for George III when those upstart colonists
revolted in 1783. "So now, Your Majesty, what about having me posted to an MTB?"

*HMS **Menestheus**, minelayer.*

There was a bright side to the minelayer posting. My
friend, David Lightbourn, was also ordered to join the *Menestheus*. We were curious and uncovered a few facts about
the ship.

> *Menestheus* was built in 1929 in Dundee, as a
> sister ship to the Agamemnon, also built in
> 1929 in Belfast. Each was 460 feet in length,
> 60 feet in the beam and capable of a speed of
> 14 knots.
>
> In Greek mythology Agamemnon and
> Menelaus (Menestheus) were the two sons
> of Atreus, King of Mycenae. In due course
> Menelaus became King of Sparta. The two
> brothers play important roles in Homer's
> Iliad and Odyssey; Menelaus, stranded in
> Egypt, survives an adventurous voyage back
> home.

In 1939 the Admiralty requisitioned both ships for conversion to minelaying. Large ports were cut in the stern and tracks fitted the length of the deck. Mines stowed in the holds below were hoisted by electric winches. Anchors were attached, the mines then rolled aft on the tracks and dropped over the stern.

Menestheus survived a bombing attack early in 1941, while minelaying south of the Faeroes. Again, in 1942 she was damaged by bombs off Iceland and towed by the Agamemnon to Lochalsh for repairs.

During 1942 she was based in Kyle of Lochalsh, nationally important as a minelaying base and the port of entry for mines. The intention was to lay a line of mines across the North Sea, thus hindering German access to the North Atlantic.

As Kyle of Lochalsh was also a naval base a submarine net was installed, to prohibit the entry of U-boats. This steel net or boom could be drawn aside like a curtain to form a gate. Further deterrents were barrage balloons which could be quickly raised into the air by steel cables, operated by winches.

David and I slept in our seats during the night journey through England, disturbed at times by joining and departing passengers. The day journey through Scotland was a constant delight. I was fortunate to have a window seat facing forward and marveled at the variety and beauty of the landscape.

The train ran along the shores of lochs with steep cliffs on one side and deep water on the other. Then with a change in the rhythm of the train engine we climbed steep slopes and emerged to sweeping views of distant mountains and down again through deep glens, with seemingly endless forest.

As we went further north we ran through heather covered moorland. Seemingly desolate, it was as uplifting to the spirit as the more flourishing land to the south. Even on these wind swept slopes there was evidence of a rich wild-life. We glimpsed elusive red deer, wildcat and mountain hare. A large bird in the distance might have been a golden eagle. Ptarmigan and grouse, the prey of golden eagles, were plentiful.

In the late afternoon we descended into Kyle, on the north shore of Lochalsh, with the village of Kyleakin across the Narrows. The area had long been considered the quintes-sential Scottish hidden gem, with railway connection to the south since 1890.

The railway station was near the waterfront. We found the office of the Resident Naval Officer who arranged that we be taken to *Menestheus* anchored out in the Bay. Once aboard, we looked back toward the shore. The little town with its background of mountains invited exploration. It was not to be. We never set foot on Kyle again.

A leading seaman showed us to the sleeping quarters, a spacious area which stretched across the entire sixty feet width of the beam. It was a pleasant contrast to the crowd-ed quarters in Gosport and Portsmouth.

After stowing our gear we were interviewed by the cap-tain, Commander Angus MacDonald RNR, a man of about sixty with the manner of a friendly uncle. Casual in dress, he was quite prepared to dispense with the formality often affected by pukka R.N. Officers.

He had no need to be affected, as he had a natural authority which, combined with his friendliness, invited obedience, instead of demanding it.

David and I were immediately at ease and handed in our C.W. Files. It was the custom for Cadet Ratings to take their files from one naval establishment to another; always securely sealed, of course, to avoid peeking at the contents.

A short conversation ensued and we learned that Commander MacDonald had spent a lifetime at sea. He had commanded the *Menestheus* since her launching in 1929, through the conversion to a minelayer in 1939.

When dismissed, we left to explore our new home. Already we felt more at ease on a minelayer. The coveted Motor Torpedo Boat suddenly seemed less desirable.

We were on board several days before taking on mines. During this period David and I were assigned galley detail, skills we had perfected in our early weeks at Portsmouth Barracks.

Once at sea, we both became lookouts. David was given the important and coveted assignment of lookout in the crow's nest, fifty feet above the bridge. With another lookout, I was usually assigned to the bridge, at the beck and call of the Officers of the Watch. When not staring through binoculars I was given vital tasks, like making hot cocoa. The trick was to keep it hot while going through long corridors and up two ladders. Covering the containers with my balaclava was a great help. Wrapping his cold hands around a hot cup earned me kudos from the Duty Officer.

I imagined complimentary notations on my resumé. "Potato peeling: Excellent, Making cocoa: Excellent." Surely I was destined to be a Rear Admiral at the very least.

My aptitude as a lookout must have been noteworthy as it was an assignment that followed me to another ship.

Mines were always primed two days before sailing, thus setting the stage for a potential holocaust. On a fateful day in 1940 the minelayer Port Napier loaded with 560 mines reported fire on board. To make matters worse she was being refueled at the same time. Had she blown up, Kyle would have ceased to exist. Kyle and the surrounding areas were quickly evacuated and the ship towed into the uninhabited Loch na Beast, where she was sunk. After the war the site became a tourist attraction and on glass bottom boats the Port Napier can be viewed, lying deep on the seabed.

To avoid air attacks the laying of mines took place at night. On the mining deck electric winches hoisted the mines from the storage hold, specially trained crews placed them on a railway track and rolled them aft. At the appropriate time anchors and chain were attached and the mines trundled over the stern into the sea.

I did not take part in the laying process but, as a lookout on the bridge, I was aware of meticulous attention by the Officer of the Watch to keeping the ship on an absolutely straight course. The same speed was also observed throughout the operation. This resulted in the mines being laid in a straight line and at regular intervals.

When returning from laying mines and in safe waters, discipline on the bridge was quite often relaxed. The Officer of the Watch sometimes disappeared into the chartroom, ostensibly to check the course, but I suspected, to have a short kip.

On one such occasion I was manning the bridge voicepipe when David called from his station, "Crow's nest to bridge."

Adopting my version of the Officer of the Watch's accent I responded, "Bridge to crow's nest, Officer of the Watch speaking."

David's reply came with appropriate deference, "Ship bearing starboard twenty-five degrees, sir."

Being already aware of a friendly ship in that position I replied, "Thank you Lightbourn. Jolly good, carry on."

Still respectful, David responded, "Aye, aye, sir."

Reverting to my normal voice I said, "OK David, you can relax now, this is Chester."

A long silence; then, "OK Chester, I'll get you for that."

David and I were now well settled on the *Menestheus*, admired our friendly Captain and had a good rapport with the other officers and crew. Not that we had a choice but we were content to serve out the obligatory sea time on *Menestheus* before, hopefully, being sent ashore to go before an Admiralty Selection Board. But after just six weeks our service on the *Menestheus* came to an unexpected and abrupt end.

I was off watch, asleep in my hammock, when we were awakened by a slight jolt, followed immediately by an alarm bell. The lights below were still on and we made our way to our lifeboat stations on the main deck. The motors were throbbing but the ship was not moving.

After about an hour we were instructed to return to our various quarters. In due course we were informed that there had been a freak accident. The *Menestheus* had run into a portion of a torpedoed ship, still afloat but just beneath the surface. Even in daylight it would not have been visible. No one was to blame.

The Damage Control Crew acted promptly, shutting off the appropriate compartments so that incoming water was contained in the bow area. The ship could proceed, but at a much slower speed. A portion of the bow at sea level had buckled and was ripped so extensively that it could not be repaired in Kyle.

As we were already at the northeast corner of Scotland near John O'Groats we were ordered to proceed to London for necessary repairs. Accompanied by an escort we proceeded south at about seven knots. The voyage was uneventful and after several days we arrived at the Royal Albert Docks on the Thames.

David and I were given weekend liberty before being sent back to Portsmouth Barracks to await another posting. We still required more sea time to qualify for examination by an Admiralty Selection Board.

On board *Menestheus*, based in remote Kyle, we had not been ashore for six weeks and now, suddenly, we were in London. So it was with great glee that we donned our No. 1 uniforms and set off for the West End of London. Having checked in at the Strand Palace Hotel, David, better acquainted with London, suggested that we spend the evening at the Covent Garden Opera House. This pre-war world famous venue for opera was now a dance hall and reputably the hangout for hundreds of dance partners. We wanted to check it out.

Just inside the entrance door a railed balcony overlooked the dance floor, six feet below. David led the way. At the railing he turned back to me and said, "Chester, my boy, we've died and gone to heaven." Joining him, we looked out on a sea of pretty girls. They swayed in their party dresses to soft music played by a small orchestra. The lights were low and the scene so far removed from our months of spartan seaboard life that we looked at each other in wonderment.

The girls vastly outnumbered the men and hundreds stood

or sat without partners at tables on the sidelines. "So what do you think, Thompson?" said David.

"Well, the odds are about right," I said, "twelve to one."

David, an excellent ballroom dancer, soon found a partner. With smooth Peabodys and other refinements of the then popular foxtrot they easily out-performed the other dancers.

I sat chatting with Elsie, whose friend, Mary, was David's partner. The four of us were soon great friends and danced the evening away. Like twin Cinderellas they had to leave before midnight to get on the last train to their home on the outskirts of London. We walked them to the station, said our good nights and then took a taxi back to our hotel.

The next day was a sunny Sunday. After breakfast we walked the Strand to Trafalgar Square. Nelson's Column, attended by two bronze lions, rescues the square from being just a sunken traffic island, infested by greedy pigeons. It is, however, a focus for visitors and Londoners alike and probably the best place in London for people - and pigeon-watching.

From Trafalgar Square we walked through the grandiose Admiralty Arch and looked for a mile dead straight down the tree lined sweep of the Mall to Buckingham Palace.

Our destination was St. James Park and we spent the morning there beside a tree lined lake with its varied wild fowl. We were comforted to see several Bahama duck.

We returned to Royal Albert Docks on Monday to collect our gear. Captain MacDonald and most of the crew had left. The once bustling ship's corridors were empty. While eager to move on I would retain fond memories of a happy ship and the avuncular Captain MacDonald.

Menestheus had lain a record 23,000 mines but was soon to have a strange twist in her career. In late 1943 conversion into a recreation ship began. She was eventually equipped with what was called the "Davy Jones Brewery," the world's only floating brewery. Some of the commodious deck space was converted into recreation halls, a theatre and cafeteria.

The plan was to have an amenity ship and provide entertainment wherever there were large groups of soldiers or sailors. Conversion was protracted and a single voyage to Hong Kong and Shanghai was made before war's end and re-conversion to a merchant ship.

CHAPTER 10

HMS Beverley

On returning to Portsmouth we were given accommodation in the Cadet Rating section of the Barracks and settled in to await being sent to other ships. The next day I met Commander Reid who was interested to hear of our adventures on the *Menestheus*. Many thousands of sailors had gone through Portsmouth Barracks during Commander Reid's tenure and we were touched by his interest in our particular careers, a nautical Mr. Chips who never forgot his students.

A conference of merchant captains at Liverpool, Summer 1941, before setting out in convoy for North America during the battle of the Atlantic.

In just a few days I received orders to proceed to Londonderry in Northern Ireland and report to the Captain of *HMS Beverley*. This was one of fifty World War I destroyers acquired by Prime Minister Churchill from the United States for the Royal Navy, in a crafty deal with President Roosevelt. Ostensibly an exchange for the lease of bases in the British West Indies, including Bahamas, it was evidence of the United States desire to help Britain in her peril.

By railway, ferry across the Irish Sea to Belfast and thence to Londonderry, I arrived to find that the *Beverley* had left port on December 3rd, two days before. The Resident Naval Officer arranged accommodation for me.

I was told that another Bahamian was in Londonderry and, to my delight, was met by Thomas Sweeting, who had arrived a few days earlier. His ship, *HMS Swale* had also left port before his arrival. We were joined the next day by Cadet Rating Tony Hart, also destined for the *Beverley*.

It was to be a long wait. The *Beverley* did not return until January 8th. Our duties at the R.N.O. Office were perfunctory and, in our opinion, a waste of time.

H.M.S. BEVERLEY

One of 50 World War I Distroyers obtained by Britain in Lend-Lease Deal with the United States. Beverley saw service in various theatres and was torpedoed by U-Boat 188 in April 1943 during North Atlantic Convoy duty.

The tedium was relieved when we discovered the Londonderry Library. Mrs. Dooley, the Head Librarian, a motherly lady in her fifties, not only introduced us to the history of

Londonderry but took us into her home. Her husband and two young daughters were welcoming and we enjoyed being part of the family.

We had time to explore our surroundings. Londonderry stands on a hill and the old position of the city is surrounded by a wall, a mile in circumference. Its former name, Derry, comes from the Gaelic word "doire" meaning "oak grove." It fronts on the Foyle, a broad estuary into which flow several rivers. North of the city the estuary widens but, after several miles, narrows again before exiting into the open sea.

When World War II began the Foyle Estuary quickly assumed strategic importance as a naval base. Convoys, originating in Liverpool and other ports on England's West Coast, completed their formations in the open sea north of the Foyle Estuary, before proceeding westward.

While we were enjoying the hospitality of Londonderry the *Beverley* was enduring the longest period spent continuously at sea. She had left Londonderry on December 3rd, as part of an escort for a Convoy of forty ships. Reports of a U-boat pack ahead resulted in a change of course south, toward the Azores.

When turning north again the weather worsened and for the next two days and nights they battled through a hurricane described by the Shore Station in Newfoundland as "the worst in human memory." Hurricane force winds blew across the Atlantic from Newfoundland to Portugal, scattering convoys and damaging ships and escorts.

One of the *Beverley's* four funnels was blown down, lifeboats swept away and guard rails bent to the deck. She limped into the shelter of St. John's harbour with the funnel secured to the deck and barely enough fuel for five hours steaming.

The crew were busy with repairs until Christmas Eve. The people of St. Johns shared everything they had and it was declared by some of the crew to be the finest Christmas of their lives, apart from the fact that they were far from home.

They sailed from St. Johns on Boxing day, December 26th to join the east bound Convoy HX 220. For six days they were buffeted by a nor' easter, ran short of fuel, refueled in Havlfjord in Iceland and finally arrived in Londonderry on the morning of January 8th.

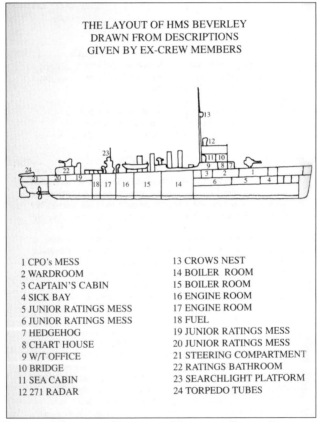

THE LAYOUT OF HMS BEVERLEY
DRAWN FROM DESCRIPTIONS
GIVEN BY EX-CREW MEMBERS

1 CPO's MESS	13 CROWS NEST
2 WARDROOM	14 BOILER ROOM
3 CAPTAIN'S CABIN	15 BOILER ROOM
4 SICK BAY	16 ENGINE ROOM
5 JUNIOR RATINGS MESS	17 ENGINE ROOM
6 JUNIOR RATINGS MESS	18 FUEL
7 HEDGEHOG	19 JUNIOR RATINGS MESS
8 CHART HOUSE	20 JUNIOR RATINGS MESS
9 W/T OFFICE	21 STEERING COMPARTMENT
10 BRIDGE	22 RATINGS BATHROOM
11 SEA CABIN	23 SEARCHLIGHT PLATFORM
12 271 RADAR	24 TORPEDO TUBES

Tony Hart and I were dismayed by our first glimpse of the *Beverley*, huddled against the dockside, looking wounded from her recent voyage. We reported to the Officer of the Watch. I was allocated to the Forward Mess and Tony to the Aft Mess. This splitting up of accommodation for ratings was a good idea the Americans had built into their ships. Should the bow be hit by a torpedo half the crew might survive.

HMS Beverley. One of fifty World War One detroyers in "Destroyers for Bases" deal with the United States.

HMS Beverley alongside at Londonderry 1942.

When built for service in World War I the ships' complement numbered eighty; now, twenty years later the *Beverley's* complement was 160. There were not enough bunks so the latest arrivals would sling hammocks wherever space could be found. It was a case of living, literally, "cheek by jowl[3]."

[3] In early use, six hundred years ago, when expressing close intimacy one said, "cheke bi cheke." Two centuries later someone substituted the French "jowl" for the second element. However, it still means "cheek by cheek.

The *Beverley* was in port just two days and left on January 10th to once again cross the Atlantic as part of an escort for Convoy ON 161.

CHAPTER 11

First Voyage - Derry to St. Johns

The last hawser, connecting the ship to the dock, was cast off. Farewells had been exchanged and our friends were already moving away. Mrs. Dooley looked around and gave a final wave. The space between ship and shore widened and the *Beverley* made her way down the narrow and tortuous River Foyle.

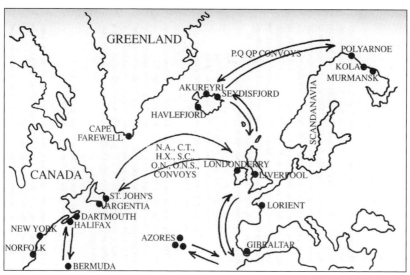

*Convy routes, **HMS Beverley**.*

From the doorways of peaceful little cottages still figures gazed at our passing. A horseman, crossing a hillside, paused and waved. Soon we rounded the last bend in the river. Our speed increased and wind keened through the rigging. The *Beverley* rode up long Atlantic swells and then gently down. The smell of the sea was all around us.

The coastline of Ireland merged into the eastern horizon. Up ahead sky and sea became one, a menacing grey void into which we headed. The wind increased and the *Beverley* struggled up the crests and made a plunging descent into the troughs. Spray covered the bow and water sloshed on the foredeck.

Soon we overtook several tired looking freighters, wallowing along, returning to North America for more essential cargoes to feed and arm a besieged Britain. Other ships appeared out of the descending darkness and took their places in the forming convoy.

We were joined by other escorts and, like sheep dogs, harried the gathering merchantmen into station. The moving lines grew longer and finally all the solitary parts became one; merchantmen and escorts banded together to defy the enemy. Unless bad weather kept the U-boats submerged some ships would not survive this running of the gauntlet.

We were taking part in a maritime exercise that had been around for centuries. In its 41st Article the Magna Carta of 1215 promised merchants safe escort of their cargo-laden ships, to and from English ports. During the intervening centuries, England's insular situation and resulting dependence on imports, had firmly established the system.

There had been a lapse of the convoy system in the First World War, which resulted in horrible losses. At the beginning of the Second World War a convoy system was put into operation immediately. Unfortunately, at first there were very few escort vessels. As a result, in the early part of the war merchantmen suffered appalling losses to U-boats[4].

In due course a frantic building programme of escort ships and development of U-boat detection devices changed the odds. But until mid-1943 the U-boats would have the upper hand[5]. It had been almost too late.

My duty was that of lookout, on the starboard side, on a slight elevation above the bridge. As protection from the cold air I was clad in long underwear, thick woolen trousers, several sweaters and two pairs of long woolen socks tucked into sea boots. Over all this, I was muffled into a duffel coat and peered through the eye slits of a woolen balaclava. I wedged myself against the steel siding so that I could better sweep the binoculars along my assigned sector of horizon.

Peering into the darkness I had time to assess the stark reality of my situation, aboard a vulnerable ship on a perilous ocean headed toward deadly enemies. I was able to summon a calm resignation. Even if I could, I would not wish to remove myself, so it seemed sensible to resolve to do my best whatever might happen. Now suddenly I was caught up in the adventure I had sought. This voyage would not only reveal new areas of ocean and land, its dangers would hasten self-discovery.

Later, I wondered if my composure was due to the daily rum ration, which I'd saved and gulped before coming on watch. Was the naval custom of "Up Spirits" keeping my spirit up? Certainly, in the frigid temperature, it kept my body warm.

The port lookout, seventeen-year-old Peter Lawrence, was struggling to stay upright and also scan the horizon. In order to join the Navy he'd claimed to be eighteen. He'd told me earlier that his only exposure to the sea was a

[4] For 1942 alone, in the Atlantic and Arctic areas, 1,027 Allied ships were sunk by U-boats, a gross tonnage of 6,348,204. In the same period only 85 U-boats were sunk. For the Allies an unsustainable average of 12 ships were lost to just one U-boat sunk.

[5] After April 1943 the situation changed dramatically. By war's end 3,000 Allied ships had been lost for 780 U-boats sunk. The ghastly score during the Battle of the Atlantic was 4 ships lost to one U-boat sunk. Thirty thousand seamen were killed.

childhood trip to Southsea. He remembered being seasick on a ferry ride to the Isle of Wight. Even though he lived inland some atavistic compulsion of his island race had persuaded him to join the Navy, instead of the Army. For Peter, the winter storms of the North Atlantic would be a cruel baptism.

On this voyage the U-boats and their prey faced a common enemy, the weather. An entry in the diary of Admiral Doenitz, Commander in chief of U-boats, reveals his concern with the weather: "The elements seemed to rage in uncontrolled fury and allowed limited contact with the enemy."

*HMS **Beverley**, December 1942 storm, lost funnel.*

Winds of up to 150mph were recorded. During the period October 1942 to February 1943 there were more than 100 days when winds reached gale strength and higher. During January alone, four merchant ships went aground, eight foundered and forty were heavily damaged. One rescue ship simply turned over and sank with the weight of ice which had formed on the decks and superstructure. The escorts suffered as well. Of the ships under operational command fewer than 70% could be kept operational at one time.

The weather was impartial and storms meant fewer encounters with U-boats. Our enemy, at least, could seek calmer waters below. On the hostile surface we struggled on across the Atlantic, sometimes losing contact with the ships we were escorting.

Breaking waves, at times higher than 100 feet, kept us partially submerged. Our movements were limited to desperate clinging to life lines. We were told later of a seaman on another ship who, having been washed off the foredeck, was miraculously washed aboard again onto the after deck.

Our progress was an endless nightmare. A short nap in sodden clothes tied into a swaying hammock was a luxury. Many of the ship's complement were seasick. My friend, Peter Lawrence, was ill throughout the voyage. There was little we could do for him. Cleaning up his vomit was done with great difficulty.

After several days of uninterrupted storm the convoy was in disarray. The transport ships were trying to survive and often lost contact with the escorts. It took skill and endurance just to head westward, however slowly. In their efforts to bring about some order the escorts used great quantities of fuel. Commander Price tried twice to connect the *Beverley* to a tanker.

The technique of fueling at sea was perfected over many months, by trial and error. At first it was simply by means of a floating hose towed astern of a tanker, picked up and connected to the fueling system of the ship astern.

This gave way to the "trough" system. The ship, requiring fuel, steamed alongside the tanker. Hoses were rigged with loops in them so that if the ships surged apart the hoses would not part. The manoeuvre required utmost vigilance, to maintain the proper distance apart and the exact relative speeds. It could be accomplished in very heavy weather but there were limits.

The conditions were now so appalling that even our skilled commander found it impossible to refuel. Being perilously low on fuel, we headed to Iceland. Our destination was a British base, Havlfjord, about 25 miles from Reykjavik the capital.

As we came into the safe and calm harbour we gazed ashore in wonder. The land was bleak and snow covered but it was solid and unmoving. Shore leave was not feasible but we were content to walk around a deck that stayed beneath our feet.

I persuaded Peter Lawrence to walk around the foredeck. His gaunt face and dark circled eyes were shocking proof of his ordeal. He had lost weight since leaving Derry. My efforts during the voyage to ease his misery seemed to have thrust upon me the role of confidant. We were on the foredeck leaning on the railing, looking across the calm waters to snow covered hills. Peter said, "There have been many times in the last few days that I wished to die." It was said with such deep resignation that I could not speak for a minute. He gazed shoreward and waited for my response. I was silent and he continued, "If I'm still alive, I'll leave the ship when we return to Derry. I'll go to neutral Ireland, it's just across the border."

I had been seasick as a teenager and explained to Peter that, in due course, he would probably become accustomed to the ship's motion. He looked at me with disbelief; he had endured such misery that my remarks brought little comfort. I later learned that the tendency to be seasick can be deep-seated and chronic.

At that moment we were interrupted by an announcement,

"Special sea duty men to your stations, stand by for leaving harbour."

"We'll speak later," I said to Peter and hurried away.

The second day out from Iceland brought worrying barometric predictions. It was our misfortune to be in the path of another storm matching the severity of that experienced when the fourth stack was blown down. It is awesome to contemplate, but the appalling weather from Derry to Iceland was to be, by comparison, a mild prelude.

That second night, and still 1500 miles from Newfoundland, the elements went berserk. The storm struck in the darkness with a fury beyond the experience of anyone on board. A terrible screeching noise was heard, increasing in volume until the wind smashed and ripped into the *Beverley*.

I was off duty but sleep seemed impossible. With nothing to keep me occupied, I was terrified. The mess deck was soon flooded and clothing and spare gear washed around. The temperature dropped and, fully clothed, I wormed deeper into my sodden hammock and tried to shut out the violent sounds of waves slamming into the ship.

The night seemed endless and sketchy sleep brought a vivid terror-filled nightmare. The ship had sunk and I was drifting downward into an abyss to join ghostly lost sailors in a vast undersea graveyard. On awakening I was chilled to the bone but wet with perspiration from my frightening dream.

As we approached Newfoundland the storm abated but the temperature dropped. Snow came in a whirling blizzard and it was deadly cold. Ice formed quickly on the superstructure. All hands available were put to work, chipping the ice away, to avoid a fatal listing and capsize. I wondered if the temperature in the Bahamas was its usual winter low of 60 degrees Fahrenheit.

The coast of Newfoundland finally appeared, a forbidding shoreline of unbroken high cliffs, toward which the *Beverley* headed. At the last moment, with the chief coxswain at the wheel, the *Beverley* straightened, speed was increased and we ran through the narrow entrance into St. Johns.

We could almost reach out and touch the sides of the cliff. The entrance opened up into a wide and welcoming harbour. Houses strung along the waterfront and marched upward into surrounding snow-covered hills. This was to be our haven for several days.

CHAPTER 12

The Sinking of U-boat 187

There's a welcome on the breeze, blown
inland from the sea,
That some folks find hard to understand.
You'll never be alone, when you're in a
Newfie home,
There'll always be a chair at the table for you
there.

(From a Newfie song)

The sentiments expressed in the song were soon confirmed. The people of St. Johns opened their hearts and
homes to us. Exposure to such kindness helped us forget
our arduous voyage and renewed our commitment to face
the dangers, which lay ahead. These surrogate families,
also attuned to the rhythms of the sea, helped allay home-
sickness for my own distant islands.

Dockyard repairs of minor damage allowed an unusual
amount of daily shore leave; sometimes we were allowed
to stay ashore overnight. Most of us soon found "homes
from home" and were fed and entertained. If we did not
show up for a meal our new friends would seek us at the
dockside.

Peter Lawrence often joined me ashore. Midwinter snows
covered the surrounding hills so we were confined to walking on the steep and narrow streets of the town. The architecture was that of a frontier town; homes built to survive
the fierce winters. For Peter and me it was sufficient to be

on land; solid, immovable, dry land.

I introduced Peter to my new friends. Their company was just what he needed and he seemed to forget the miserable voyage from Derry to St. Johns. I avoided any reference to our conversation in Iceland when he spoke of deserting to neutral southern Ireland.

I thought of Annabel often and hoped that mail was awaiting me in Derry. Better yet, if shore leave was given there might be a chance for us to meet. But now, with a wide and dangerous ocean between us, I would have to be content with memories to sustain me, in the cold dark watches ahead.

At the end of January we were ordered to join an Escort Group guarding Convoy SC118. Somehow, several of our friends knew of our departure and were at the dockside. The Bosun's voice echoed throughout the ship. "Special sea duty men to your stations. Stand by for leaving harbour."

The last rope was taken in and we moved slowly away. My friends on the dock shouted:

"Safe voyage, Tommy."

And, "Come back, 'Bahamas' to your northern out-island."

They gave a final wave and soon merged into the background of dockyard buildings and snow-covered hills.

We went through the narrow channel with steep cliffs looming on both sides. From my lookout position it seemed that I could reach out and touch the land. And then, suddenly, we were in the open sea; our speed increased and the *Beverley* began her now familiar rolling progression, an old drunken lady emerging from a lighted pub into a darkened street. I took a quick look astern and already the land had blended into the murky sea and sky.

During the next 12 hours we overtook and joined Convoy SC118: 64 merchant ships from New York and Halifax, laden with essential cargoes, without which England would collapse. Included in the convoy was *SS Henry R. Mallory* carrying 384 troops. As usual, our speed was that of the slowest ship: seven knots.

Convoy forming up in Halifax Harbour, 1942.

The Escort Group consisted of three destroyers, four corvettes and the U.S. Coast Guard cutter, *Bibb*. An important addition was the British *SS Toward*, the first of two specially designed rescue ships, with accommodation for several hundred survivors, an R.N. surgeon and a well staffed sickbay. Rescue gear included a big dip-net for picking up water soaked and oil-smeared survivors.

Just before dawn on February 4th a foreign merchant ship in the convoy accidentally set off a Snowflake, a brightly burning powder fired in a rocket. It enabled merchant ship gun crews or escorts to sight any surfaced U-boats, inside the columns.

U-boat 187, acting as scout, was a few miles away and immediately alerted two nearby Wolfpacks, the Pfeil Group and the Haudegan Group, a total of 24 U-boats. This was to be the beginning of several days of almost constant encounters with U-boats. The diary of Admiral Doenitz, recovered after the war noted, "The battle around Convoy SC-118 was perhaps the hardest convoy battle of the War."

But U-boat 187 was to be the first victim. Its sighting report was detected by *SS Toward*, equipped with the latest High Frequency Detection Finder, H.F./D.F., abbreviated by the Navy to HuffDuff.

The *Beverley* was alerted. "Action Stations," was piped and we all scrambled to our assigned posts. Captain Rodney Price took command on the bridge. The Chief coxs'n was at the wheel. As usual I was Starboard Look-Out.

Dawn soon came and, as ordered, we ranged ahead of the Convoy. Other escorts took up positions on both sides and astern of the Convoy. It was nearing 1100 hours when the mast-head look out sighted U-187, on the surface, about 12 miles ahead. We closed at our best speed. The Convoy Commodore was informed and *HMS Vimy* was sent to assist.

As the range closed Captain Price decided to attack with the forward 4 inch gun. Unfortunately, this was not possible as the target appeared only occasionally when we were both on the crest of waves.

As expected, in the meantime, the U-boat submerged. Then at 1235 hours, in company with *HMS Vimy*, we located the enemy with our Asdic[6]. Both ships now attacked

---

[6] Asdic: An anti-submarine detection device, after 1947 known as Sonar.

with depth charges[7] and Hedgehogs[8]. The *Beverley* went in first, with *Vimy* standing by as consort, about 1000 yards astern.

It was necessary to be slightly ahead of the target before dropping the depth charges, thus allowing for movement of the enemy below and the sinking of the charges. Meticulous judgment was required of the Captain as the Asdic signals were lost about 300 yards from the target.

Depth charge station and explosion.

[7] Depth Charge: A drum shaped underwater bomb, ejected from the stern when over the target. The depth at which it exploded could be controlled so it would be as effective as possible.

[8] Hedgehog: This was the first weapon to throw its projectiles forward, thus allowing submarine detection devices to be effective until the last moment. Used from 1942, the weapons were situated on the foc'sle between the bridge superstructure and the forward gun.

I was looking through my binoculars in great excitement when Captain Price shouted, "Fire." I saw the charges arcing through the air and splashing into the sea. Twenty charges were dropped, set to explode at various depths. The resulting explosions rocked our ship.

In the meantime the *Vimy* had closed the range with the U-boat's position and also attacked with Hedgehogs and depth charges. The U-boat could not escape and to our great excitement was forced to surface. It appeared to be down by the stern. The crew were seen clambering through the conning tower and leaping into the sea. There was tumultuous cheering from our crew. I was filled with a savage delight.

Then occurred one of those rare moments which sometimes define extraordinary events and is framed in memory for a lifetime. Rodney Price, our Captain, looked upward to my look-out station and directly into my eyes. For a brief moment we transcended the gulf between Captain and Ordinary Seaman. He smiled and winked and gave a mock salute, which I returned. Our ship and crew had beaten a deadly and determined enemy.

The crew of a sinking U-Boat swimming for their lives.

This was the reward for countless days and nights of fear and frustration, of thousands of miles steamed, sometimes in weather so appalling that survival seemed impossible. But on this remarkable day we had been in the right place at the right time.

At this point *HMS Vimy* went off at high speed to investigate a suspicious area. We set about picking up the U-boat survivors now swimming toward the *Beverley*.

A scrambling net was let down the starboard side and our crew stood by to help the Germans on board. As the first swimmer grasped the scrambling net he was pulled backward into the water by the swimmer immediately behind. A member of our rescue crew could not restrain himself and shouted down, "What the f--k are you doing?"

Survivor being helped up scrambling net.

The swimmer was hanging on to the net with one hand while holding his hat firmly on his head. We learned later that this was the Commander of U-187, Ralph Muennich.

He had decided that he should be the first of his crew to face the enemy rescuers. This had been his first command and was to be his last, as he was a prisoner-of-war until hostilities ended.

We had rescued 41 bedraggled and sodden Germans when *HMS Vimy* came storming back at full speed, signalling frantically, "Don't be greedy, leave us a few." She then picked up the remaining seven. Nine had died during the attack.

Picking up U-Boat survivors.

U-187 was now slowly sinking by the stern. The *Beverley* and *Vimy* hastened her demise by several well placed shots from the 4-inch guns. She quickly sank lower, the bow up-ended and she slid into the depths. There was loud cheering from the crews and despondent looks from the Germans, not yet confined below.

Without detracting from praise due to *HMS Vimy* it is thought that official reports of her role in the attack over-shadowed that of the *Beverley*. The *Vimy's* gallant commander had been awarded a Victoria Cross for previous exploits and was therefore better known at the Admiralty than our equally skilful commander, Rodney Price. It is sufficient that their teamwork resulted in one less U-boat.

The German prisoners were confined in an unused boiler room and brought on deck for short periods, in groups of ten or twelve, when weather and other conditions were suitable. Armed sentries stood guard. Conversation with them was forbidden.

On one such occasion, Max, one of their number, ventured, "We don't want war," and, pointing at us, "you don't want war but Churchill wants war and Hitler wants war." We did not respond. They were the enemy. Though they were unarmed and shuffling around the cold deck, we were wary.

As I stared at Max, I remembered that on the first day of the War a U-boat sank the passenger liner *Athena*, with the loss of 112 civilians, continuing their murderous record from World War I when, on May 7, 1915, they torpedoed the liner *Lusitania*, with the loss of 1150 lives including 50 babies and 100 other children.

CHAPTER 13

A Decisive Battle

Official records detail the continuing battle between U-boats and Escorts during the next four days. A shortened version follows:

> The sighting report of the now sunken U-187 resulted in orders from Grand Admiral Doenitz. Seven U-boats concentrated around the convoy with plans to attack on the night of the 4th.

Grand Admiral Karl Doenitz (1891 - 1981), commander of the German U-boat fleet and from January 1943 of the German Navy, here, congratulating Lieutenant Otto Kretschmer, a U-boat 'ace' of the Atlantic battle.

> Their almost continual transmission and sighting reports were monitored by the escorts, who charged down the HF/DF bearings and drove off the U-boats, including U-

267, U-402, U-608 and U-609.

During this maritime melee, around mid-night, the Convoy Commodore ordered a change of course. In the confusion three columns of merchant ships were separated from the main Convoy. Most of the U-boats followed this section but were unable to exploit the situation, due to the vigilance of the escorts.

An Atlantic convoy changing course under orders of its commander during the Battle of the Atlantic.

On the morning of the 5th the two sections of the Convoy joined. The weather now deteriorated and for a while the U-boats lost contact. The American *SS West Portal* had engine problems, lagged behind and was sunk by U-413 during the night.

There was now a brief respite, and normal watch keeping routine allowed some desperately needed rest. The convoy was reinforced by three American escorts from Iceland.

By midday on the 6th the U-boats returned, and again the escorts were at Action Stations. There was now air cover and U-465 was badly damaged by a Liberator. *HMS Vimy* put U-267 out of action but the sister U-boat 266 sank *SS Polykter.*

In the early evening of the 6th, six U-boats attempted attacks but were driven off. Later that night U-262 got through the escort screen and sank *SS Zogloba.* All hands perished but they were avenged when U-262 was badly damaged by U.S. Coast Guard *Bibb* and *HMS Lobelia.*

U-Boat and victim.

Up to this point, the escorts, though hard pressed, were well in control but they now had to deal with a German ace, Baron Siegfried Von Forstner, in command of U-402. Shortly after midnight U-402 moved in and sank *SS Daghild* and *SS Toward* and then retired to reload.

The loss of the rescue ship *SS Toward* was to have serious consequences as the escorts were now responsible for picking up survivors. But leaving the convoy to pick up survivors made it easier for U-boats to sink other ships.

Baron Forstner in U-402 took advantage of this and in company with U-boat 608 sank an oil tanker. Then he slipped astern of the convoy and sank two stragglers. From one of these, the troop ship *Henry A. Mallory*, there was heavy loss of life including almost all the 384 troops.

Air patrols now flew over the Convoy and U-boats were prevented from surfacing. U-624 dared to do so and was sunk by a B-17. During the night of the 7th, U-456 was driven off by the *Beverley* but Baron Forstner sank his seventh ship with his last torpedo.

Considering the determined and sustained attack by the U-boats our loss of only 12 ships out of 64 was considered favourable. The nationalities of the 12 lost ships reveal the diversity of the nations opposing Hitler: five British, three American, two Greek, one Polish and one Norwegian. But 80% of the Convoy made it into port with their vital cargoes. Three U-boats were sunk and others damaged.

For the past three years U-boats had ruled in the Atlantic. Allied efforts, with appalling loss of life and ships, seemed futile. For many months the number of ships sunk by U-boats exceeded 100. Thus deprived of food and war materials the valiant Britain was being brought to her knees.

The battle around Convoy SC118 marked the beginning of

a turning point in the Battle of the Atlantic. By the end of April 1943 improved offensive use of HF/DF and radar made it difficult for U-boats to make surface attacks by night and submerged attacks by day. Admiral Doenitz now ordered his U-boats to keep as far away from the convoy as possible during the day and to make only submerged attacks at night. Increased air cover from Iceland, Northern Ireland and Newfoundland now closed what had been a "vulnerable gap in mid-Atlantic."

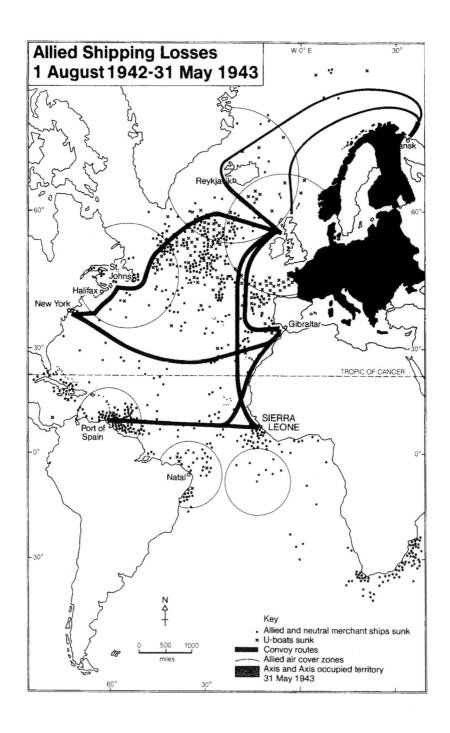

**Allied Shipping Losses
1 August 1942-31 May 1943**

Reykjavik

St. Johns
Halifax
New York

Gibraltar

SIERRA LEONE

Port of Spain

Natal

TROPIC OF CANCER

N

0   500   1000
miles

Key
•   Allied and neutral merchant ships sunk
×   U-boats sunk
━   Convoy routes
⌒   Allied air cover zones
▨   Axis and Axis occupied territory
     31 May 1943

CHAPTER 14

The Jaws of Death -- Three Episodes

On board the *Beverley* the reality was not as orderly as the official report might suggest. From the perspective of a crew member the four day battle was an endless chaotic ordeal, with sudden alarms, explosions, changes of speed and ships burning in the night. A chronological account is not possible.

Terror was always lurking. It could be controlled by concentrating on one's assigned task. Also, there was the survival instinct of youth, a feeling of invulnerability, a denial that death was seeking you – maybe the other person, but not you. Being one of a team was a great stimulus to courage. Better to die than to let your shipmates or yourself down.

Sixty years later several episodes are vivid, against a background of darkness and confusion. These are evoked when least expected; by a chance remark, rough seas, a cry in the night or witnessing the uncomplaining endurance of pain.

There was the night the *Beverley* was sent to rescue survivors from a sunken freighter. On the way, contact with a U-boat was made. The pinging sound of the Asdic was audible on the bridge. The U-boat could not be far away. A report was made to the Convoy Commodore.

"Action Stations," was called. Captain Price increased

speed as the *Beverley* headed down the bearing toward the U-boat. The Asdic operator reported that the U-boat was turning to the left. The *Beverley* followed.

As the *Beverley* sped across the darkened ocean we were suddenly in the midst of tiny bobbing red lights spread across the sea. Faint voices were heard crying for help. Our headlong rush to the U-boat had brought us into the midst of the survivors we had been sent to rescue.

It happened so suddenly that before the Beverley could decrease speed we had ploughed through the survivors. Bodies were seen being cast aside by our white bow wave. Very quickly the cries faded as the swimmers were left astern. We increased speed toward the enemy. The rules of combat were clear. Engaging the enemy had priority over picking up survivors.

In the end the U-boat eluded the *Beverley*. Depth charges were dropped with no result. For the next two hours a search was made. Our Asdic was unreliable in waters already disturbed by depth charge explosions.

It was finally concluded that the U-boat had gone to the maximum depth of 230 meters and moved away on an unknown course. On reporting to the Convoy Commodore we were ordered to return to our position to close the gap in the convoy, through which an alert U-boat might slip.

Death would have come quickly to the survivors we passed in the night. Survival time in the frigid waters, even for the most hardy, was of short duration. Buoyed by their life vests the bodies would drift and sway in a macabre dance, before slipping downward to join uncounted dead, in a vast under sea graveyard, casualties of this long and far flung battle.

And there was an awful night that long after was still intensely vivid. The dreadful truth is that such scenes from hell were played out many times during the long and cruel Battle of the Atlantic.

One of the twelve ships lost from Convoy SC118 was an oil tanker. It was targeted by U-boat 402 and U-boat 608, no doubt, because of its vital cargo. Without oil Britain's war machines were useless. At night the two U-boats attacked simultaneously. Torpedoes from both hit the tanker. In seconds the tanker was on fire from bow to stern. The ocean and sky were illuminated, creating an amphitheatre from hell. The *Beverley* raced to the scene.

Torpedoed oil tanker.

Burning oil, which had engulfed the tanker, now gushed into the surrounding sea. The *Beverley* kept at a safe distance to avoid being also engulfed by flames. There was no way to help. We could not long remain silhouetted by the flames, an inviting target for a U-boat.

We assumed that no one could have survived the gigantic explosion. As we were turning away we saw, to our amazement, that four survivors were swimming away from the main conflagration.

Oil, spreading across the sea, was on fire and moved faster than the swimmers. At first, the doomed men seemed unaware of the approaching flames and swam bravely on. We watched helplessly as one by one they were overtaken and became alight. They flung their limbs around violently before dying.

We were now moving away and gazed in shock at their charred and blackened bodies. Not one escaped. I became aware that I was holding my breath and clutching my binoculars, as if trying to crush them.

And then there were the two Dutchmen, the toughest men I've ever known. Their courage was of a higher order than that needed for a confrontation with an enemy. Facing an enemy, one has the impetus to perform a particular task, the fulfillment of a responsibility and the examples of courageous companions.

The incredible courage of these two men lay in their quiet, unbreakable spirit and their refusal to take the treacherous hand of death, when death smilingly offered release.

The *Beverley* had been sent to investigate an area north of the convoy. The required box search took all morning. Only then was Captain Price satisfied that the suspected U-boat was not there. We were now on our way to rejoin the Convoy.

It was very cold, the sky a thick canopy of grey cloud. We were running through long flattened swells. As there was little spray some of the off-watch were on deck, well protected in duffel coats from the cold. Peter Lawrence, now between bouts of seasickness, joined us on the after deck.

A tiny smudge on the horizon was spotted by the port lookout. It was not a ship from the Convoy, as we still had some considerable distance to run. To guard against U-boat trickery the Captain ordered, "Action Stations."

As we approached, the speck took shape and was seen to be a ship's lifeboat. We soon came abreast. The hull was scarred and looked as if it had been adrift many days. Two ominously still figures were in the stern sheets but as we approached one raised a hand. Then turning to the other he appeared to be trying to awaken him.

The captain brought the *Beverley* alongside. Three of our men scrambled down into the lifeboat. The two men were helped aboard and taken to the sick bay.

Two days later they were allowed on deck for a short while. My friend, Tony Hart, and I were detailed to help, as they were still quite weak.

Both were in their fifties. Alain, the older, spoke English well; Hans depended on Alain to communicate. They were both from a small town on the Dutch coast. Both had survived previous torpedo attacks. Alain spoke of their ordeal calmly and with impressive understatement. He may have been speaking of an unpleasant sailing holiday off the Dutch coast.

His ship had been battered by a storm for several days and forced to drop out of the Convoy. When the storm passed and while attempting to rejoin the Convoy the ship was torpedoed. It was at night. Alain and Hans, having learned from a previous sinking, slept fully clothed. They grabbed extra clothing - duffel coats and sweaters - and rushed on deck. The ship was already listing to starboard. Men were shouting and jumping into the water. The ship still seemed to be moving slowly ahead so the swimmers were left astern.

There were shudders, minor explosions and the frightening sound of inrushing water. The ship sank lower. They were joined by two younger men who had rushed from below, clad only in their underwear. Together, they attempted to free a lifeboat. Their combined efforts failed because of twisted davits and tangled ropes.

The ship was sinking lower, the sea just a few feet below the lifeboat. They threw themselves into the boat and cut the restraining ropes. The boat dropped and the resulting splash drenched the four but the boat remained upright. There were four oars and they rowed quickly away from the ship. In spite of the exertion the two younger, ill clad men were now suffering from the below zero temperature. Alain and his friend shared their warm clothing with them. They were not aware of the ship sinking below the waves but suddenly they were alone on the dark ocean.

Then began an uneven contest with the cold, which quickly sought out the movement and supply of their blood. First their feet and hands became numbed. Alain and Hans continued rowing, directionless but with determination to push back the final deadly grip of cold.

The younger men cried to the empty ocean for help. They cursed and moaned at intervals, which grew longer, as increasing cold offered the treacherous release of sleep. By morning their lifeless bodies lay stiff across the thwarts.

After dawn, came feeble sunlight and a small measure of warmth. Alain and Hans took turns standing, while the other provided support. The sea had calmed and they could thus, feebly at first, move their feet and legs in a walking motion.

They sang in cracked voices, started telling jokes only to forget the punch lines. Together, they remembered the words of a sea burial service for their dead companions, first recovering their warm clothing.

They were without food and the available water was used sparingly. In turn, they took short naps, one staying awake to rouse the other. Thus the day passed and another long night, while they kept their grip on life.

Then another day with no sign of a ship on the vast ocean. By the third day it became more difficult to stay awake. That afternoon the *Beverley* came in sight. Alain recognized the four stacks of the ex-American destroyer. By shouting and prodding he was able to rouse Hans, from the sleep of death.

CHAPTER 15

Return to Derry – 1st Voyage

O captain! My captain! Our fearful trip is
done,
The ship has weathered every rack, the prize
we sought is won,
The port is near, the bells I hear, the people
all exulting.
The ship is anchored safe and sound, its voyage is closed and done.

Walt Whitman

The ships we had protected, as well as most of the escorts, were destined for Liverpool. After our eventful voyage together, they seemed like old friends. As we changed course for Londonderry signals were exchanged with the other escorts. The Convoy Commodore signaled the *Beverley*, "Farewell to the old and the bold. Well done."

Later in the day the coast of Northern Ireland came into view. We were soon in the familiar waters of the Foyle Estuary and began our passage up the narrow and twisting river. Every bend revealed stone-walled fields and wooded hillsides, with the ancient walls of Derry beckoning in the distance. Children waved from cottage gardens. Gazing at these peaceful pastoral scenes we felt enfolded in a safe embrace. For a brief time we were removed from the wide Atlantic, with its cruel storms and deadly U-boats.

While approaching the docks our officers and men changed into their No. 1 uniforms. The German prisoners were blindfolded, brought on deck and lined up on the port side. We would be docking port side to, so that the prisoners would be in full view from dockside.

Blind folded prisoners of war disembarking at Londonderry.

This provided a triumphant homecoming for the *Beverley* and crew. But equally important, dockyard workers and others, who provided support on shore, shared in this brief moment of glory. Often unrecognized, the dockyard workers were important links in a chain that kept our ships afloat and equipped to deal with the enemy when found. Or, more often, when they found us.

Some of our crew were detailed as guards. The Germans were helped down the gangplank and marched off to begin their processing as prisoners of war.

Then we had our first showers since leaving the Caribou Hut in St. Johns, two weeks before. Here, in Derry, a row of showers took up an entire inside wall of a building. Unlimited hot water provided one of life's greatest pleasures, as we literally washed away the grime and ashes and pains and, symbolically, the submerged fears of our ordeal at sea.

Fortunately, my watch was granted shore leave and I was able to accept a dinner invitation from the Dooleys. Their home on a hill near the church had been a haven for me, while waiting to join the *Beverley* in early January.

It was a delight to sit around the warm fireplace and be one of the family. Maureen, the Dooley's oldest daughter, was home on leave. She was a pretty girl of medium height with abundant black hair, which fell to her shoulders. Her face was lovely, with high cheek bones and green eyes with long lashes.

All went well until Maureen was told of our humane treatment of the German survivors. Then, directing her remarks at me she shouted, "Why didn't you churn them up in the propellers? The bastards deserve to die." I was astonished and watched helplessly as, tearful and trembling, she ran from the room, her face contorted with emotion.

Mr. Dooley explained that Maureen's dear friend was lost a few weeks earlier when the oil tanker on which he served was torpedoed. There were no survivors. Maureen was, forgivably, quite embittered.

She returned in a few minutes and, still tearful, said to me, "I'm sorry I shouted at you. I know you're blameless. I'm just angry and desolate and fed up with this wretched war."

Mr. Dooley diplomatically spoke of other matters and when dinner was over Maureen appeared composed. Turning to me, she said, "I need to walk and will walk with you to the ship." I said, "I'd like that, but only if I walk you back home."

We laughingly agreed that instead of going to the ship we would walk along the cobbled pathway on the inside of the circular wall, which surrounded the old city. This would bring us back to her home.

It was a fine night and a few stars struggled through the winter sky. As we walked in the shadow of the looming wall, Maureen spoke of the loss of her friend. It was evident that she needed a symbolic shoulder on which to cry, while she coped with her grief.

They had known each other as children and then, by chance, met again at a course in Signals. They planned to announce their engagement when he returned from the fateful voyage.

He died in the most hideous manner known, in an ocean rife with monstrous deaths. In the long history of warfare with its noble sentiments: "dying gallantly," "lay down your life for your country," and Tennyson's, "into the jaws of Death, into the mouth of Hell," there can be no greater travesty than the horrible deaths of torpedoed oil tanker crews in the Battle of the Atlantic. It will forever rank with the senseless carnage of trench warfare in World War I; the darker side of mankind. Maureen was struggling to comprehend the incomprehensible.

Now here in this safe land, under a starlit sky, with a tearful Maureen beside me speaking of her friend's death, I was for a moment back on the *Beverley*, clutching my binoculars and watching as swimmers from the torpedoed oil tanker burned in the flames. My eyes too filled with tears. I turned to Maureen and we held each other.

The shadowed old wall looked on. For three hundred years it had witnessed mayhem, courage, grief, compassion and mankind's enduring spirit. These had not changed.

Our walk ended on the steps of the church, Maureen's home just a few doors away. She reached up and kissed me on the cheek. "Thank you," she said, "you've helped me a lot."

As she walked away I said, "You'll never know how much you've helped me."

She paused and turned, "I'll pray that you get back to your beautiful Bahamas," she said.

I watched until she opened her door. She turned and lifted her hand in farewell. It would be long after, by a bizarre twist of fate, that our paths crossed once again.

CHAPTER 16

Moonlight and Cloud Shadows

The next day we were told that all hands would have a week's leave. I spent the morning trying to contact Annabel and finally succeeded, through her parents.

They phoned at noon with the good news that Annabel had arranged a long weekend pass and that I would be welcome at their home in the village of Albury, in Surrey.

I had not seen Annabel for five years, when we were both sixteen. I was in a state of high excitement and slept fitfully that night. By first light I was on the train to Belfast. Thence a ferry ride across the Irish Sea and by train to London.

We had agreed to meet under the clock at Liverpool Street Station. I was early and stood beside a news kiosk. Headlines boldly announced "ROMMEL AND MONTGOMERY CLASH." The platform teemed with people hurrying purposefully in various directions; numerous Army, Navy and Air Force uniforms, a manifestation of Britain's resolve to wage war, whatever the outcome.

The minute hand of the nearby clock did not seem to be moving. I mused on the gamut of humanity that, over the decades, had used the clock as a rendezvous: friends and lovers, knights and knaves, rich and poor, men and women of good will and opportunists looking for victims.

And then I saw Annabel emerging through the platform gate. Though now transformed into womanhood, the lineaments of the graceful teenager I remembered were unmistakable. Even encumbered by a shoulder bag she moved with the same quick dancer's stride, feet seemingly not touching the platform.

I waved; she smiled and came slowly toward me. As she approached her blue eyes looked directly into mine. She was lovely, her oval face framed by blonde unruly curls. I was trembling and walked to meet her. We embraced for a long time, oblivious of the jostling crowd.

The journey by underground to Waterloo station passed in a blur. We held hands and spoke continuously, trying to catch up on our five years apart. Most of our remarks began with, "Do you remember?" "Do you remember when we picked seagrapes?" "Do you remember when we fished for turbots?" We spoke of happy times on those innocent Bahamian islands, in their warm seas, when the world was at peace. It all now seemed as remote as the stars.

On boarding the Guildford train we found an empty compartment. As other passengers paused at the door I discouraged their entry by pretending the onset of apoplexy: looking wildly into their eyes, contorting my mouth and emitting deep-throated whimpering sounds.

It worked. As the train shunted out of the station we were alone and fell about with laughter. I said, "I owe you at least five kisses." She came close, put her arms around me and said, "And much, much more."

The train's mournful whistle warned of our passing through crowded London suburbs. We held each other and found that we could both fit easily on one seat. For a long time there was no need for words.

The train was now running through the fields and woodlands of open countryside. I remembered that Annabel had been traveling since early morning. "Try and sleep,"

I whispered.

She stirred and then turned and kissed me, "That's a good night kiss. Yes, I am tired" she said. She tucked my hand in both of hers, put her head on my shoulder and promptly fell asleep. I found this immensely endearing and was content to close my eyes and rejoice in her nearness.

Annie and Bill, Annabel's parents, met us on the platform at Guildford station. Annie hugged us and said, "We're happy you could both come." Bill shook my hand and said, "You're almost as tall as your father." I remembered that in Abaco they had shared a love of sailing.

We were soon in the car and heading for their home on the outskirts of the village of Albury. At times we seemed to be motoring through a shallow sea of rising mist. Tenuous strands crept up the hillsides. Soon it was dark and much colder. It was a joy to arrive at their home and warm ourselves around the fireplace.

After our long journey it was decided that after dinner we should be early to bed. We sat briefly with our coffee in front of the dying fire. Annabel gave a noisy yawn, which resulted in an involuntary yawn from me. "I think it's time you two went to bed," said Annie. Bill was reading a newspaper and, without looking up, said, "Yes, it's time that you both go to your bedrooms." Annabel looked at me with a rueful grin and a slight lifting of the brow.

I shook Bill's hand, kissed Annie and Annabel on their cheeks, and climbed to my bedroom on the second floor. I opened a window and looked out into darkness. It was very cold. I quickly burrowed under the bed covers. Annie or Annabel had been at work and the bed was thick with blankets and an eiderdown cover. I was soon blissfully asleep.

The weather changed during the night and I awoke to a cloudless sky. I joined Annie and Bill in the cosy breakfast room. A bay window looked out to the back garden. Welcome sunshine brightened the forlorn rows and hinted at an early spring.

Over coffee we spoke excitedly of the day ahead. Bill was taking the day off, a rare event, as he was dedicated to his medical practice. This gave us the opportunity to have an outing together and use of Bill's car; an important consideration, as petrol was severely rationed.

We were joined in the breakfast room by Annabel, still in pyjamas and dressing gown, looking sleepy eyed and cuddly. I found it difficult to concentrate on the conversation.

While Annabel and Annie packed a picnic lunch Bill and I planned our day. We would motor to the nearby North Downs with its chalk land slopes and beech groves, mostly protected by the National Trust. There would be attractive picnic places, forest and wildlife trails and, if we felt up to it, a climb up Leith Hill, at 965 feet, the highest point in southeast England.

As we set off the sun was beaming down, benignly warm for February. Woodland creatures were deceived and we saw foxes peeking from hedgerows and rabbits running for cover.

We headed for Coldharbour, a village on the eastern side of Leith Hill, where we parked and began our ascent. It was fairly strenuous but without time constraint we paused often to rest and admire the view. On reaching the summit we climbed an 18th century tower. From the top there were panoramic views of surrounding woods and farmland, becoming hazy with distance, as hills and valleys merged and marched eastward into Kent.

It was long past noon when we returned to the car. The picnic lunch was soon eaten. Not having packed drinks, we sought refreshment in The Plough. We were in a relaxed holiday mood. "I bow to circumstance," said Bill, rushing through the doorway.

We were soon sampling the ale and resting from our climb. For Bill and me one pint led to another. The girls preferred shandigaff, a mixture of beer and ginger beer. Before long we were in that "jocose" stage of inebriation, when even serious remarks seemed funny.

English pubs seem to be frequented by "characters". One of this special breed joined our table, clutching an empty glass. He introduced himself as "Jack the Stripper" and said that he would accept a pint.

He had chosen the right table. Bill and I were in a benevolent mood and if asked would have bought drinks for everyone in the pub. With a full glass in hand, Jack the Stripper told us that he performed as a stripper every Thursday night at a Home for Aged Women in Kent. While of advanced years, he looked sufficiently fit to be a stripper but it was obvious, even in our haze of generosity, that he was pulling our legs in order to quench his thirst.

Accounts of various exploits as a stripper followed, including a Command Performance at Buckingham Palace. His glass always needed a refill.

At some point he became curious about my transatlantic accent and asked the inevitable question, "Where are you from and what do you do?" I welcomed this opportunity to pay him back in kind.

I explained that my family lived near Apalachicola, Florida. For three generations we had been chicken farmers. Studies had shown that chicken legs were preferred by all three individuals in three member families. My father, recogniz-

ing a business opportunity, had through selective breed-
ing, produced a three-legged chicken.

Jack the Stripper looked at me impassively, expressed
admiration for my father's scientific achievement and reminded me that his glass was empty.

I was being kicked under the table by Annabel and said to
Jack "It's now your turn to buy us drinks, but first let me
tell you more about my father. Encouraged by his success
with the three-legged chicken, my father went on to pro-
duce a rooster that laid eggs."

There was a long silence from Jack the Stripper and then,
still without speaking, he left, clutching his empty glass.

Annie and Annabel said that Bill and I were "tiddly" and
that it was time to leave. Annie said, "Bill, darling, I think
I'll drive."

Annie said that she and Bill had another commitment and
that, on our last evening together, Annabel and I might
like to dine at a nearby restaurant. I was touched by her
thoughtfulness and suspected that she was fibbing about a
commitment.

It was a beautiful clear evening, with promise of a full
moon, as Bill drove the two miles to the restaurant. As we
got out of the car Bill said, "Annie and I will not go to bed
until midnight."

As we walked down a short path toward the door I said to
Annabel, "Was that meant to be a curfew?"

"You know my dad well," said Annabel with a laugh.

Before entering, we walked in a landscaped garden surrounding the restaurant. Bordered pathways with arbours
and statuary were now illuminated by hidden lights. We
sat on a bench at the end of a pathway and held hands as
twilight gently deepened into darkness. We remembered
one of Annabel's favourite poems by Rupert Brooke and,
with roosting birds as an audience, quoted:

> Tenderly day that we've loved, we close your
> eyes,
> And smooth your quiet brow and fold your
> thin dead hands
> The grey veils of the half-light deepen, col-
> ours fade
> I bear you a light burden, to the shrouded
> sands.

On entering we were shown to a cosy lounge. A wood fire
and soft lighting made the room most welcoming. Hunting scenes and old weapons on the walls gave a feeling of
stepping back into another century.

We were alone and sat on a couch facing the fireplace. Annabel's face was exquisitely lovely in the soft light. I covered her hand with mine and we gazed into the fire. The
ever-shifting flames invited introspection. Annabel suddenly turned to me and said, "What will happen to us?
When will this terrible war end and how will it end?"

I said, "We must believe with all our heart and mind that
we will win the war. Until then we can only do our best."

Annabel moved closer and turned her face to mine. There
were tears in her eyes. "I know that when we part you're
going back to a very dangerous place," she said. "I must
believe with all my being that you will come back to me."
I leaned closer and we kissed. Her lips were welcoming,
face and hair wonderfully fragrant.

We were shown to a corner table in the dining room. Candlelight and a warm fireplace made the room cheerful and inviting. The Dover sole we had previously ordered was now served. The waiter brought a bottle of chilled white wine. He said that it had been sent by a friend, who would be identified after dinner. Puzzled but grateful we toasted our mysterious friend.

Before our lives were changed by the war we had both dreamed of attending universities. We now spoke of our interest in English literature and made a solemn pledge that we would not abandon our dreams. We so enjoyed being together that without being aware, the dining room emptied and it was time to go.

When I asked for the check our waiter said, "It is all taken care of, including wine and gratuity. Dr. Lee phoned and said you were his guests." We thanked the waiter.

Annabel said to me, " We should have known."

We had dined well, were warmly clad and decided to walk home. Once away from the restaurant the road wound through high trees. Moonbeams flickered through the branches and we walked in a shadowy ethereal light. An owl flew by on silent wings.

Soon the trees gave way to fields, bordered by elm trees. We were now in full moonlight. The road led upward. We took a vote and decided unanimously that a short rest was needed and sat with our backs against a haystack, just off the road.

Cloud shadows raced across the field and merged into darkness under the elms. "It's my turn to quote Rupert Brooke," said Annabel.

> Down the blue night the unending columns
> press

In noiseless tumult, break and wave and
flow
Now tread the far South, or lift rounds of
snow
Up to the white moon's loveliness.

Her face was near to mine and I said, "Annabel, I love you.
I loved you from the very first time we met."

"And why was that?" she said.

I thought for a minute and said, "Well, you're a good
climber of seagrape trees, you know how to catch turbots
and you scull a dinghy like a man."

"Is that all?" she said, stuffing a handful of straw down my
collar. A friendly scuffle followed but soon we were holding each other as if it would be forever.

Tenderness enveloped us and we murmured and laughed
and cried with joy and the moon began its downward journey. Some time passed and then through my euphoria, as
insistent as a bosun's whistle, I remembered Bill's thinly
veiled injunction, to be home before midnight.

"Annabel, we must go, right now," I said. "Your father will
shoot me before the Germans do." We were nearer home
than we realized and had time to sit for a while with Annie
and Bill and thank them for dinner.

CHAPTER 17

Second Voyage

There gloom the dark broad seas...
...the deep moans round with many voices.
Tennyson

By the end of February 1943 the *Beverley* was on the move again to join Convoy ONS169 which left Liverpool on February 24th, with 37 merchant ships. On the 26th we made our way down the now familiar Foyle Estuary, smoke from cottage chimneys on the shoreline a reminder that we were leaving warm hearthsides for the bitterly cold Atlantic. Greeted by fierce gales we joined the Convoy to complete its escort of three destroyers and four corvettes.

Immediately, on February 27th, one day into the voyage, we ran into a fierce southwest storm and were forced to reduce speed. The next day the wind shifted to the north-west. Several ships were damaged, including the Asdic dome on *HMS Highlander*.

These gales which lessened the threat from U-boats played havoc with the limited number of escorts. When ships arrived in port, maintenance facilities worked at full pressure to repair damaged ships. It was regarded as a crisis by Admiral Horton of Western Approaches Command and he wrote:

> The whole war situation depends on the number of escorts available to protect convoys...I urge most strongly that the highest

priority be given to refitting and that no departure be made from this policy.

*Admiral Sir Max Horton,
commander, Western Ap-
proaches, a former subma-
rine officer who directed the
Battle of the Atlantic from
the British side, 1942 - 1945.*

By the night of March 3rd the storm was at Force 10. This
continued for the next five days. The *Beverley* rolled fu-
riously; enormous waves higher than the superstructure
threatened to engulf us, but miraculously, each time she
would rise from the onslaught, tons of water pouring in
torrents off the decks.

Watch keeping was a nightmare; hanging on to a life line,
awaiting the right moment to begin the ascent of a slippery
ladder and finally strapping oneself into the lookout position.

The mess decks were awash, spare gear and clothing un-
derfoot, broken crockery, nowhere to rest except in a satu-
rated hammock. Cooking was impossible and for days we
subsisted on tea and corned beef.

It seemed that the storm would never end. When not on
watch the long hours dragged by, to the sound of howl-
ing winds, creaking of the superstructure, continual breaking away of something or other on deck and tramping and
voices of men changing watch. And always the cold, sub-

zero temperatures and, on deck, blinding snow flurries.

By March 6th we were off the southern tip of Greenland. The bedraggled remnants of the Convoy, speed reduced to three knots, battled Force 11 winds amid icebergs and drifting ice floes.

Orders were received to make an evasive turn to the west but the *Beverley*, low on fuel, was allowed to make straight for St. Johns, Newfoundland.

On the way we ran across the tanker, *Empire Light*, a straggler from the previous Convoy ON168. Two days previously *Empire Light* had been torpedoed by U-boat 638, but was still afloat.

We risked a brief searchlight view of the stricken ship and, by loud-hailer, informed the six remaining crew members that we would return. Commander Price then did a search in the surrounding area for U-boats.

Then occurred a defining never-to-be-forgotten event. Commander Price with unexcelled seamanship and exceptional bravery attempted a rescue of the six men. With the search light on the men, now crouched waist deep in water on the fast sinking ship, Commander Price shouted, "We cannot lower a boat so be prepared to jump."

He then brought the *Beverley* alongside the *Empire Light*, with both decks heaving in the swell, one rising as the other fell. With remarkable coordination of helmsman and engines Commander Price kept the ships in a relative position so that the men could jump. It must have taken immense courage to jump and to decide when to do so, as the ships rose and fell in forty-foot waves.

Five of the six men made it. The sixth clutching an empty rum bottle refused to jump. Fearful of damage to the *Beverley* and aware that we were an easy target for a U-boat, our captain had to leave.

The rescued men, including Captain Lewis, were not seriously injured. We had padded the foredeck with bunk mattresses and some of us stood by to help break their fall. Four days later we were in St. Johns and they were taken to hospital for a short stay. Captain Lewis was full of misgiving that he had broken the maritime tradition of the Captain being the last to leave a sinking ship. I was told later that Captain Price convinced him that under the circumstances he was blameless.

One of the survivors, 18-year-old Bryn Morgan, later wrote an account of the last days of the Empire Light. A shortened version follows:

> We were late leaving Liverpool but caught up with Convoy ON168 the following day. As we progressed westward the weather deteriorated with rough seas and falling snow. It got so cold that normal four-hour watches were decreased to two hours. Most of the crew were seasick.
>
> Four days out the *Empire Light* suffered engine failure and came to a standstill. The Convoy carried on. We were lashed without mercy by great waves. The next day the engine was repaired and we caught up with the Convoy. The weather got continually worse.
>
> Three days later the motor failed again and could not be repaired. The Convoy sailed on. We were in dire trouble. The starboard lifeboat was washed away by heavy seas and ice formed on the deck.
>
> A request by wireless to St. Johns, 350 miles away, to send a tug could not be granted as

the weather was so bad.

At 12:30pm on March 6th a passing U-boat could not resist a sitting target and torpedoed the *Empire Light*. Ignoring orders from Captain Lewis, some of the men boarded a lifeboat and cut it loose. It crashed into the sea and was soon smashed against the side of the ship. All the men died.

There were now just six of us left alive. As succeeding bulkheads gave way the ship settled lower in the water.

Twenty-four hours later at midnight the *Beverley* appeared. At first we thought it was a U-boat and were relieved when an English

Oil-covered survivor

voice asked us to identify ourselves.

We all prepared to jump, as ordered, except a seaman who had been drinking for the last twenty-four hours. We did our best to persuade him to make an effort. It was useless.

When it was my turn I closed my eyes and jumped. The next thing I remember is coming to in a bunk and Captain Price saying, 'You are now safe on board the *HMS Beverley.'*

I returned home to Britain in June 1943 and felt privileged to live the rest of my life because of the brave act of the captain and crew of the *Beverley*.

The *Beverley* continued the voyage to St. Johns, impeded by vast fields of ice floes. Continuous chipping away at ice on the superstructure lessened the danger of capsizing.

Astern of us Convoy ON169 struggled on in the relentless storm. Two of the remaining escorts, the corvettes, *HMS Pennywort* and *HMS Sherbrooke*, also low on fuel, made straight for St. Johns. Five merchant ships straggled from the Convoy. By March 9th the Convoy's speed was down to 2 knots, practically hove-to.

Two destroyers, *HMS Montgomery* and *HMS Salisbury* arrived as reinforcements, which released the damaged *HMS Highlander* to head for St. Johns for urgent repairs.

That night U-boat signals were picked up by the rescue ship Gothland. Fortunately, next day the weather improved and air cover was provided by a United States Navy Catalina.

The storm battered remnants of ON169, destined for U. S. ports, did not reach Cape Cod until March 19th, after 22 days at sea. The Admiralty report on the voyage of ON169 was characteristically succinct but surely tongue-in-cheek. It was described as a "peaceful passage."

Going through the narrow channel into St. Johns and tying up dockside was an awakening from a dark and evil nightmare into a warm, safe and well lighted room. Our friends were waiting with their generous offerings of entertainment and meals.

The *Beverley* soon swarmed with workmen, putting in long hours to make us shipshape as soon as possible. In particular, the fourth stack, blown down and repaired two voyages previously, needed further reinforcing.

Liberty men, without special "homes from home" were always welcome at the Caribou Hut. Named after the well-known symbol of Newfoundland, it provided a homely atmosphere for thousands of Canadian, British and American servicemen. It opened in 1940 and closed in June 1945.

In 1997, on the fifty-seventh anniversary of the Caribou Hut opening, Bert Riggs, a Newfoundland archivist, wrote:

> It was a place of fun and relaxation, of good food and laughter. It was a place to dance and spend a romantic evening with a young Newfoundland woman. It was a place to fall in love and a place to say good-bye; some lasted only for an evening or until the next casualty list; others for a lifetime.
>
> Imagine what it must have been like in the 1940s. What a kaleidoscope of colours; sailors in their Navy blue and white, strolling

up from the waterfront; the khaki green of
the Army and the blue of the Air Force, the
gold braid of the Officers, the multi-coloured
dresses of the young women, the music and
the dancing; mouth-watering odours wafting
from the kitchen.

St. Johns was a place to renew the spirit, to provide a
warmth, that lingered in memory when one again faced
stormy seas and a ruthless enemy. And for the survivors,
lifelong memories of a kind and generous people.

To echo a Newfie song:

There's no price tags on the doors of New-
foundland.
So raise your glass and drink with me,
To that island in the sea,
Friendship is a word they understand.

While the *Beverley* was undergoing repairs and the crew
recovering from their ordeal with Convoy ON169, another
group of ships was forming in New York and Halifax for
the voyage to Britain. This was to be one of the largest
convoys of the war and was divided into Convoys HX229,
HX229A and SC122. Lying in wait were three wolf-packs
code-named "Raubgraf" ("Robber Barron"), "Dranger"
("Harrier"), and "Sturmer" ("Attacker"), 42 U-boats in all,
outnumbering our escorts by more than two to one. Even
more important was the enemy's foreknowledge of the
convoy's movements.

With repairs complete, *Beverley* joined HX229 on March
17th and immediately went to help *HMS Volunteer* which
had been attacked by a U-boat. The U-boat was driven off
but in the meantime a surfaced U-boat went through a gap

in the convoy and sank the merchant ship *Elen K.*

The *Beverley* was ordered to pick up survivors form *Elen K.* While on the way other orders were received to rejoin the convoy, as two merchantmen, *James Oglethorpe* and the *Zoanland*, had been torpedoed. I have no recollection of survivors from these three ships.

Later on the night of March 17th a U-boat contact was made 3,000 yards astern. Turning, the *Beverley* decreased speed to eliminate the bow wave. Three minutes later radar contact was lost but two minutes after that there was an Asdic contact.

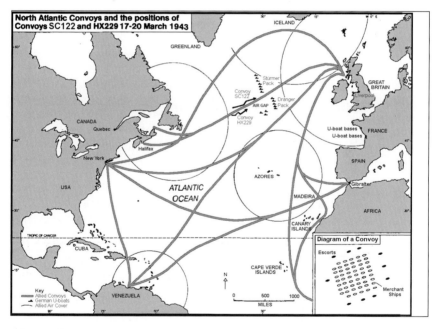

The U-boat was moving rapidly to the left, the *Beverley* put on thirty degrees of portwheel. Suddenly, at 400 yards the U-boat altered course to the right which brought it inside the *Beverley's* turning circle. When the U-boat was abeam charges were dropped, without visible result. We were not to know until later that our target, U-228, on her first patrol, was damaged by the explosions and withdrew from the battle, not to rejoin it.

The U-boats were unrelenting in their attacks and the battle continued. In his book, *Battle at Sea*, John Keegan, noted military and naval historian, writes:

> The destroyer, *Beverly*, an ex-American four-stacker with a turn of speed, was meanwhile achieving one of the group's few successes of the battle. Positioned ahead of the convoy, it spotted first one, then another U-boat lying in wait, worked up to 25 knots, forced both below and quickly got a firm sonar contact on one of them. *Beverley's* crew were experienced. They had sunk a U-boat the previous month and damaged another on the morning of 17 March. They were about to subject U-530 to a submariner's nightmare: a prolonged and accurate sonar and depth-charge attack. For two and a half hours, *Beverley* made one run after another, six in all, damaging the U-boat so badly, even when it went below 600 feet, that all its lights went out and water started to enter through the torpedo tubes. 'The younger men were very steady,' a crewman recalled, 'but the married ones looked scared.' Another, more convincingly, said, 'We were all in terrible fear.' *Beverley's* final attack was with its single one-ton depth charge, which would certainly have sunk U-530 but for the firing mechanisms failing to operate. The destroyer was then obliged to return to close escort of the convoy, leaving the U-boat to struggle away, its pressure hull creaking under strain and water sloshing over the terrified crew's feet. The boat had lost almost all buoyancy, the pumps had been damaged too badly to shift liquid outboard, and it was only by violent use of the electric motors that its captain, Kurt Lange, was eventually able to force it to the surface. Not one of Donitz's more aggres-

sive commanders - he was the second oldest in the fleet - he turned U-530 for home.
Beverley's sustained depth-charging of U-530
- she had dropped twenty-seven charges and
fired two Hedgehog salvoes - had the indi-
rect effect of frightening away several other
U-boats which were shadowing. In conse-
quence, HX229 passed a quiet night.

In spite of air support from Northern Ireland and the vigilance of the escorts, by March 20th, a total of 21 ships had
been torpedoed, amounting to 20% of the ships in Convoys
HX229, HX229A and SC122.

Historians agree that the U-boat was the only weapon with
the potential to defeat Britain. The brave airmen over London in 1940 staved off immediate invasion but for 2,073
days the navies and merchant marines, with tragic loss of
men and ships, kept the Atlantic lifeline open. Without
raw materials, weapons, fuel and man power from across
the sea Britain would have been defeated.

Winston Churchill recorded in his memoirs:

> The only thing that really frightened me dur-
> ing the War was the U-boat peril. I would
> willingly have exchanged a full scale attempt
> at invasion for this shapeless, measureless
> peril, expressed in charts, curves, and statis-
> tics.

In retrospect, March 1943 was the pivotal point. Nobody,
except those concerned, knew that the fate of Britain was
on a razor's edge. In spite of storms, during the first 20
days of March, U-boats in the Atlantic and other areas sank
85 ships.

Samuel Eliot Morrison, noted historian, wrote:

> Over 500,000 tons of shipping were lost in
> 20 days. The only visible compensation was
> one submarine, U-633, sunk by a British Lib-
> erator out of Iceland. So many escorts were
> under repair that the convoy system was in
> danger of disintegrating. So many U-boats
> were out (an average of 116 operating daily
> in the North Atlantic) that evasive routing
> was futile; a convoy avoided one concentra-
> tion of U-boats only to fall in with another.
> Clearly we could not go on losing ships and
> men at that rate. When convoy after convoy
> came in with six to twenty ships missing, the
> morale of the seamen, who had to make the
> next voyage, was impaired. The patriotism,
> the energy and the sheer guts that kept these
> men of the merchant service and of the three
> escorting Navies, to their allotted task, is be-
> yond all praise.
>
> By March 21st, one may say, the crisis had
> passed. Losses were cut during the rest of
> the month and in April there was a distinct
> improvement.

By dawn of March 25th the weather had improved. The
cliffs of Malin Head, Ireland's most northerly point, were
silhouetted in the rising sun. The surviving ships of the
convoy continued through the North Channel and south to
Liverpool, to unload their vital cargoes.

The *Beverley* was released from escort duty and by noon
we were off Inshowen Head. The off duty watches were

on deck as we passed through the welcoming narrows between Green Castle and Castle Rock.

Then into the broad reaches of a calm and safe Loch Foyle, no longer the target of lurking U-boats or cruel unpredictable storms. The relief was palpable, the crew now laughing and waving to cottagers as we passed the villages of Moville and Carrowkeel. By early afternoon we were threading our way up the narrow channel and before nightfall were tied along side the dock in Derry.

Tony Hart, the other Cadet Rating, and I went to a local pub for the evening. We discussed the possibility of our leaving the ship. We had arrived in Londonderry in early December and waited four weeks for the *Beverley's* return. The two months sea time we had now served was a month short of the required minimum three months, before going before an Admiralty Selection Board, in Portsmouth. However, in my case, I hoped to be credited with the six weeks served on *HMS Menestheus*.

The next morning we were ordered to meet with the Captain. He told us that we should do one more voyage on the *Beverley*, to complete the required three months minimum sea time. He could not count the four weeks ashore waiting to board the *Beverley*.

I had to hide my disappointment that my service on the *Menestheus* was ignored. I believe the Captain had in mind that Tony and I having joined *Beverley* together should leave together; two replacements to be requested in the meantime.

It was a damned-if-you-do and damned-if-you-don't situation. The records show that we "readily agreed" to another voyage. We had no choice; any hint of dissent could result in adverse comments on our resumés.

A guardian angel was hovering nearby. Just before we

sailed, on what was to be *Beverley's* final fateful voyage, we were ordered to meet with Captain Price. He told us that the Admiralty had instructed him to release us to attend an imminent meeting of a Selection Board. He thought that a certain quota of C. W. Candidates was being sought. As we parted we were gratified when he said, "When you are commissioned please write to me, I'd like to have you on the *Beverley.*"

Before leaving I persuaded Peter Lawrence, my sea sick friend, to accompany me to a meeting with First Lieutenant David Revill, with whom I felt a measure of rapport. I explained to the Lieutenant that Peter wished to request compassionate transfer to a shore establishment; Peter's appearance eloquently supported the request. Lieutenant Revill promised to recommend the transfer to the Commanding Officer, a promise he reiterated when we chanced to meet later in the day.

We were suddenly very busy, saying good-bye to the Dooleys and our shipmates. We had a short pub-crawl with six other crew members who were leaving, including my good friend Bill Bartholomew. Bill, a RDF operator, had been training another crew member.

CHAPTER 18

Good-Bye to *HMS Beverley*

The last we saw of the *Beverley* was the view at her berth, across from the railway, as we left Londonderry. Tony and I settled in our seats as the train headed toward Belfast and the ferry to England. I knew then that my brief service on the *Beverley*, with her brave Captain and crew, would be a defining memory, to the end of my days.

Sixty years later I salute them; though suffering the miseries of life on a small ship, they remained cheerful and steady throughout, always ready to perform their duties with skill. I was privileged to serve with "souls that toiled and fought and wrought with me," as so aptly said by Tennyson.

While we were on our journey to Portsmouth the *Beverley* was preparing for another voyage. By early April she was in the North Atlantic with an escort group guarding Convoy 176.

Dense fog settled in on April 9th. Having delivered urgently needed diptheria serum to *HMS Clover* the *Beverley* returned to her station. At 10:00pm in thick fog she was in collision with *SS Cairnvalora*.

Just how it occurred will never be known. The crew of *Cairnvalora* remembered that the *Beverley* was pushed so far over that men were seen hanging on to anything to stop from sliding into the sea.

Beverley was holed on the starboard side and one of her oil tanks was flooded. The Convoy commander signaled approval for *Beverley* to proceed to St. Johns, Newfoundland, for repairs. Commander Price responded, "With your permission, Sir, I'll wait until the morning."

By morning of the 10th, twelve U-boats had been detected in the area. They attempted six attacks during the day, all driven off by the escorts. The seventh attack succeeded in the early morning of April 11th. The target was the *Beverley*; ironically the attacking U-boat was U-188, sister craft to U-187, sunk by the *Beverley* in February.

A B Horton[9], one of four survivors, remembers vividly what happened next. Survivor of a torpedo attack on the cruiser *HMS Glasgow* in 1940, Bob had a sixth sense alerting him to impending danger.

> I had just completed midnight watch and there was something too quiet about the sea. I "turned in" wearing my overcoat and boots. My mates laughed at me.
>
> Three minutes later there was a terrific explosion. The lights went out but the emergency system came on. I felt quite calm and rushed on deck. The ship was sinking fast but we couldn't free the cork life rafts. Several of my mates jumped overboard but I decided to stay on board and go down with the ship rather than freeze to death in 40 below zero sea.

---

[9] At the time of publication, Bob Horton is still alive in Windsor, England. We often exchange letters.

The ship keeled over and so great was the suction it pulled the boots off my feet. My overcoat fanned out and kept me from being sucked under. I swam breaststroke to a nearby float and managed to scramble on top.

About seven of us made it to the raft. We saw the *Beverley* stand sixty feet straight up. The next moment she was gone.

I was told later that as the ship went down she was picked up on the corvette Clover's asdic. The whole area was then mistakenly depth charged, killing many of the *Beverley's* crew.

Time ticked on and one by one the exposure caused my mates to drop off into the sea. After about two hours I was alone. Sometime later the corvette came by looking for survivors and I shouted to them, asking if they were going to pick me up or leave me to die. At one point I could touch the corvette but was told I would be picked up later on.

More time passed and I couldn't believe my eyes when I saw the corvette returning for me. They threw out a life belt and hauled me up on deck. I was given a hot bath and a tot of rum, maybe two tots. Then while I was lying in a bunk I heard the whole area being depth charged again. I thought to myself, "It is just as well they picked me up."

I was the last of four survivors and had lasted over four hours in 40 degrees below zero water. After recovering in a Newfoundland hospital I returned to sea for another three years and was demobbed in 1946.

Tony and I were not to know of the loss for a few weeks. Sixty years later we still grieve for our lost shipmates and are in awe at our last minute reprieve.

Eighteen year old chronically seasick Peter Lawrence died along with my friend Lieutenant Revill and my revered captain, Lieutenant Commander Rodney Price; making a total of 151 lives lost. Peter Lawrence's death left me with a life long dilemma. By discouraging his desertion to neutral Southern Ireland I may have saved his self-respect, at the cost of his life.

The poignancy of Peter's death was intensified when I read in a newspaper the following Memoriam:

THEIR NAME LIVETH FOR EVERMORE

LAWRENCE - In proud, glorious and ever-lasting memory of Peter Victor Lawrence, Ordinary Seaman, R.N., only beloved son and brother (Mr. and Mrs. A. V. Lawrence) who was lost on April 11, 1943, aged 18 years, together with all his gallant and heroic ship-mates of *HMS Beverley*. We sadly miss our happy "Pete" - Mummy, Dad, Eileen, Tan, Jean.

> "He was so young to give so much. A boy but brave as any man, withholding nothing, gladly and ungrudgingly, giving all they have to give that others might be safe and free."

PRICE - In proud memory of Rodney, Lieut. Cmdr. Royal Navy, *HMS Beverley*, April 11, 1943.

HMS BEVERLEY - In proud memory of the Officers and Ship's company, lost in the Battle of the Atlantic, April 11, 1943.

On arrival in Portsmouth Tony and I were accommodated in the C.W. Mess at Portsmouth Barracks. As the sitting of the Selection Board was imminent we were denied leave.

CHAPTER 19

The Selection Board

The day of the dreaded interview by an Admiralty Selection Board finally came. The waiting room was filled with nervous candidates. The tension was palpable. Many of us had not slept properly for several nights.

The stakes were high. After an interview of, perhaps, fifteen minutes one could be rejected by the Board and suffer the heartbreak of being sent back to sea as an Ordinary Seaman. The Board's approval meant beginning a three months long course, leading to a commission as a Sub-Lieutenant, RNVR – Royal Naval Volunteer Reserve. There would be various tests and exams along the way. At any time their Lordships could decide that a candidate lacked O.L.Q. – Officer-like qualities – and he would be sent to Portsmouth for posting to a ship.

There was an unintentional diabolical refinement to the Selection Board's procedure. The ringing of a bell would indicate that the candidate in line could enter the Board Room. There he was seated and faced six or seven elderly gentlemen, some in Naval uniform, seated behind a long table on an elevated platform.

The intimidating and appraising stares of seven pairs of eyes and unexpected questions were daunting for even the bravest and best prepared candidates.

The interview over, the candidate was sent to a waiting room, empty except for one chair. There one sat, awaiting the Board's decision.

A light above the door announced their verdict: if Red, you'd failed and would be sent back to sea; if Green you'd be allowed to begin the course. However, your fate would still be uncertain; one could be rejected at any time during the three months course, for failing to meet the required standards of conduct and achievement.

At times, Candidates with superior officer-like qualities would fail and, of course, some misfits would survive. It was a flawed system but it seemed to work.

I was warned that the "old school system" could be a factor in the selection process. It was said that the Board favoured candidates with an English Public School education. Would the Board approve of Western Senior School in Nassau, from which I graduated? True or not, this thought eroded my confidence. Later on I discovered that the Royal Navy of World War II, especially on smaller ships, could be surprisingly egalitarian.

When I was called and seated in front of the Board members all went well at first. I answered their questions without hesitation and with the deference due to my venerable judges. I hoped that my school background would be forgotten.

And then, an old gentleman in a tweed coat, who I'd thought to be asleep, spoke up: "Thompson, I see on your record that you went to Western Senior School. I'm assuming that Western is misspelled and that you went to Weston Senior, that fine old Public School in Weston Super Mare."

He paused. I stopped breathing. Before I could reply, another member of the Board interrupted, "Explain to me, Thompson, the significance in ship handling of 'green to green and red to red, perfect safety go ahead.'"

I replied in great detail. Other questions followed. The tweed coated gentleman had nodded off again and the Board was left with the distinct impression that I'd attended Weston Senior "that fine old school in Weston Super Mare" instead of Western Senior School in Nassau.

I've never been certain if the tweed coated gentleman was merely making a play on words or, if there was a Weston Senior School near Weston Super Mare.

The interview ended but the impassive faces of the Board members gave no indication of their decision. I thought I'd responded well to all their questions. Allied with my service on HMS Beverley and my attendance at the "old Public School, Weston Senior, in Weston Super Mare" I should make it,…but?

The clock on the wall of the waiting room seemed to be defective. The minute hand was not moving. I closed my eyes and counted to ten and then twenty. When I opened them the Green light was on. I could look forward to the challenges of the next three months.

CHAPTER 20

HMS King Alfred -- Lancing College

I was now Cadet Rating Thompson and wore a white band around my hat. Assigned to a C.W. Mess at Portsmouth Barrack, I awaited instructions. Within a few days I was sent with other Cadet Ratings to Lancing College, in the hills above Brighton and Hove.

The bus drove through beautiful grounds and deposited us at an entrance quadrangle. The buildings had been designed to accommodate boys of seven to twelve, the desks, chairs and toilets for this age group still in place. For the first few days there was a distinct Gulliver-in-Lilliput feeling.

The buildings, on a hilltop, looked across to other wooded hills. At the bottom of our hill a small river ran along the boundary and disappeared into a thicket of greenery. It was April and the countryside was awakening to the phenomenon of an English spring, for which Robert Browning in exile, lamented, "Oh to be in England now that April's there."

While aware of the glories of spring our entire attention was devoted to serious matters such as Gunnery, Torpedoes, Signaling, Navigation, Pilotage, etc.

Gunnery and Torpedoes were chores to be endured, to earn necessary marks. Signaling, Navigation and Pilotage were of great interest and I enjoyed the lectures, demonstrations and assignments.

To the amazement of some of my classmates I looked forward to drilling and march pasts. I had received such grounding in this at Portsmouth that I was usually right hand man, front row, i.e. the point man.

There were many lectures and, at first, reams of notes were taken. However, we soon learned to be judicious and stick to headings with brief descriptions. An attempt to take down every word could be counterproductive.

During the fifth week there was a cross country run. We understood that a good performance in this could balance weaknesses in other subjects. Our instructors took the run seriously and spoke of it often. During the fourth week we were taken for a walk along the route.

On Friday of the fifth week we assembled on the playing field in our running gear. At the last minute we were told that the run would include a test to measure our memory under stress.

At the moment of starting the race, an instructor would repeat a sentence just twice. We were forbidden to write. At the end of the run the sentence would be repeated to an instructor.

In the intervening sixty years I've forgotten the sentence. Indeed, I barely remembered it at the end of the run. It was something like: "Proceed with all dispatch to search, find and destroy three U-boats now 300 miles due East of Cape Farewell, Greenland and heading 180 degrees."

At first the run was downhill, a mob spread out and jostling for position. Splashing across the riverbed and scrambling up the opposite bank dispersed the runners somewhat. My strategy was to follow Cadet Taylor, said to be a county champion.

We crossed a wide field, along a lane, and then upward toward the crest of a hill. As we ran uphill I was able to pass some runners, with only Taylor ahead. When I reached the top he was already in the valley below and beginning a great circle back to Lancing. He had not increased his lead and I was content that he set the pace.

Between breaths I repeated the main points of the sentence, "three U-boats" – "300 miles East of Greenland" – "heading 180 degrees." It became my mantra.

Taylor had increased his lead and was running easily. I was struggling. As I stumbled on, pigeons flew out of the oaks and startled rabbits catapulted from the hedgerows. Sunlight filtered through blossom-laden branches.

I think that fatigue made me slightly delirious. I summoned my rugby team mates from Nassau. We were in a hard fought match on the Eastern Parade and I pleaded, "Help me, Bucky ," "Evie[10], we need a touchdown." Suddenly, Lancing was in sight on top of what seemed a mountain. I was near enough to see Taylor finish the race. And then finally I too reached the top. Taylor seemed fresh and unruffled. He shook my hand and said, "What kept you, Thompson?" I repeated my version of the sentence to an instructor, who gave a noncommittal nod and made a notation on his list.

There were examinations during the last week but our Divisional Officer seemed to place more importance on our achievements throughout the course.

It was thought that an interview with the Divisional Officer during the last week meant failure. These interviews were private and could take place at any time, even on the last morning. With our goal of a commission in sight the thought of failure and return to sea as Ordinary Seamen

---

[10] "Buck" Johnson and Everette Sands.

was distressing. It had happened to those who were, in our opinion, more qualified.

Sadly, at our final Parade there were a few missing Cadets. Selfishly, one now felt safe for another six weeks. Our final trials would be at *HMS King Alfred* at Brighton.

CHAPTER 21

HMS King Alfred -- Brighton

On a sunny Sunday afternoon I reported to the Brighton location of *HMS King Alfred* on the waterfront at Hove. The Barracks strung out along the waterfront, its draughty underground passages and echoing corridors a stark contrast to Lancing College, with its beautiful gardens surrounded by wooded hills.

It was named after King Alfred of Wessex, the first to use ships when the realm was threatened by Danes. By so doing he became the father of The British Navy.

Lancing College and Hove Marina were requisitioned by the government in 1939 and commissioned as *HMS King Alfred*. By war's end 22,500 candidates passed the course and were commissioned as RNVR officers.

The career Royal Navy officers referred to RNVR officers as "90 day wonders," forgetting long periods of requisite sea time and merciless scrutiny by the Selection Board before being eligible to take the course. The RNVR in turn, referred to the Royal Navy as "peace time caretakers."

The pace of our studies was now frantic. In contrast, the six weeks at Lancing College seemed leisurely. I have no recollection of any break in our studies at Brighton. It was all drill, marching, study and lectures.

At Lancing I had felt confident with Navigation but now at Hove our Instructors devised a devilish exercise, which made us all fearful. It was known as the "Action Plot." After the first episode we called it the "Pandemonium Plot."

Without notice, during a plotting exercise, turmoil would be staged by our mischievous instructors. We would be startled by the thunderclap of firecrackers in the aisles or under our chairs. Our desks would be shaken, often spilling charts and pencils onto the deck. The shouting, clapping, banging and clangor was enjoyed by the instructors but often left us unable to complete an exercise, because of lost pencils or mangled charts.

Lewis guns, Torpedoes and Gunnery were humbugs for which I could not summon a smidgen of enthusiasm. I dutifully learned by rote sufficient details to hopefully result in passing grades. The Gunnery manual, kept beside my bed, was a sure remedy for insomnia.

My training in Signals at Portsmouth Barracks, bolstered by practical experience on *Menestheus* and *Beverley*, gave me confidence that I would earn a good passing grade.

Training in ship handling was limited by weather and availability of a twin motored craft. In the entire six weeks at *King Alfred* I had just one 15-minute session at bringing a craft alongside.

As a child I had learned the golden rule of ship handling from my father. "Let wind and tide be your slaves - not your masters."

Lectures on ship handling were mostly a waste of time. How to bring a four mast square rigged nineteenth century ship alongside was useful only as trivia, to enliven a boring conversation.

Earning points for tying knots was a gift, "money for old rope," for anyone of nautical background.

The phoney insults of Petty Officer Pattendon at Portsmouth Barracks now paid off and I felt increasingly competent at arms drill and marching.

With just two weeks to go our already busy days were complicated by solicitations from Gieves and Moss Brothers, local tailors, eager to provide uniforms for the latest batch of officers. We optimistically ordered our uniforms for delivery on the afternoon of graduation, fully aware that this would increase the severity of our disappointment, if we failed.

The Division ahead of us were already posturing around in their new uniforms with the single gold ring on their sleeves. We would lay in wait and embarrass them into returning our salutes. On graduation day their class had suffered just six failures.

On Thursday of the last week we sat our final examinations. We started off with practical subjects: Drilling and Marching, Signals and Knot tying. The written exams were in the afternoon: Torpedoes and Lewis Guns were followed by Navigation and Pilotage. The insides of torpedoes and Lewis guns were mysteries to me and I groped for answers. With Navigation and Pilotage we were spared the Action Plot and I wrote with confidence.

The next day we gathered in the Auditorium. For most of us it would be our last day in Ordinary Seamen uniform and we did our best to look smart.

The graduation ceremony was made even more painful for those failing, by the custom of calling names in alphabetical order. The first knowledge of failure was when one's name was omitted.

Those of us in the last quarter of the alphabet suffered agonies. Halfway through, the names of Charlesworth,Gordon, Kingsley and Mowden had been omitted. I knew them all. In my opinion they would have made admirable officers, better than me with my jaundiced view of Torpedoes and Lewis Guns.

Our nervousness increased. Finally they called Taylor, who marched to the front for his diploma. Then, Templeton. I held my breath and then let it go, as my name was called next.

Coinciding with the commissioning ceremony at King Alfred my older brother Leonard arrived from Canada and was billeted at the RCAF[11] Deployment Centre in Bournemouth. We arranged to meet the day after graduation.

Leonard was at the station when my train arrived. So that we could make the most of our limited time, Leonard smuggled me into the plush hotel in which he was billeted. I was loath to change from my new uniform but a RCAF uniform of my size was borrowed from Leonard's chum, so that I blended into the crowd.

We had been apart for two years. Leonard had seen our parents just weeks before, having taken his Canadian bride, Mary, to live in Nassau. We now spoke incessantly of events at home and adventures to which we had been exposed.

It was at the end of my visit, on my departure from Bournemouth, that Leonard and I escaped death, simply because

---

[11] Royal Canadian Air Force.

we weren't thirsty. The events of that afternoon illustrate the role that pure chance plays in life.

Our language is rife with expressions describing the caprices of Lady Luck, roll of the dice, luck of the draw, the way the cookie crumbles, destiny, serendipity, etc. In wartime the whims of chance can mean life or death.

On that sunny Sunday afternoon in Bournemouth we left the hotel to walk to the railroad station. Departure time was not for about three hours so we strolled leisurely, pausing to sit in the park for a while.

On continuing we came by a pub and looked in. It was crowded, the overflow standing outside clutching mugs of beer. Everyone was relaxed and jolly. Some of Leonard's friends called for us to join them.

I looked at Leonard. He said, "I'm not thirsty."

I replied, "We just ate well, I don't need a drink." We walked on and sat on a grassy mound overlooking the station, content to sit in the sun and speak of happy times from our boyhood.

Suddenly, the Sunday peace changed to noise and confusion. Two low flying enemy aircraft approached from seaward, having streaked across the Channel at wave top height. With machine guns chattering they were shooting up the town. Leonard recognized them instantly. "F.W. 190s," he shouted, as we dove behind a concrete water trough. The planes continued toward town centre.

The planes carried 550lb bombs. Explosions were heard but in minutes the raid was over. The planes banked and again, at wave top height, disappeared toward France.

My train departure was not for another hour. We took a quick walk into town. One of the bombs had made a direct hit on the pub, a prime target, no doubt planned in advance.

The area near the pub was cordoned off. It was already swarming with rescue crews, fire engines and ambulances. We learned later that sixty people were killed and many wounded, including families with children in the nearby park.

Some years later I was told by a Bournemouth resident that this strafing was the only attack on the town, during the war.

I returned to *King Alfred* to find that most of my class had gone on leave. I was free to go as well, with the injunction that *King Alfred* must always know my whereabouts. In due course we would all be assigned to ships.

After an anxious twenty-four hours and various phone calls to Annabel we arranged to meet in London on the following Saturday morning. I then phoned Auntie Grace who immediately said, "You must come to Fordy Farm. I'm happy you're bringing Annabel and will be at Ely Station to meet the midday train from London."

CHAPTER 22

The Betrothal

Auntie Grace in a pony trap was at Ely Station to greet us. Annabel and Auntie had not met before but at once chattered away like old friends, while I retrieved our luggage.

Barney, the pony, was tossing his head, eager to be away from the noise and confusion of the station. Auntie guided Barney into the main street. I squeezed onto the back seat with the luggage while Annabel sat on the front seat with Auntie. I wasn't very comfortable, but at least I didn't have to look at Barney's swaying backside for seven miles. Uncle Whittleton was right. There is an advantage in every disadvantage.

Soon we were making our way down a long gentle slope. Before us a flat plain stretched to a wide horizon. There was little traffic and Barney settled into a gentle trot. The seven miles to Fordy Farm led us through the small peaceful village of Soham and the even smaller Barway. The two thousand acres of Fordy Farm encompassed tiny Barway.

The house, Fordy, could be seen for a mile across the flat fields. Square built and two storied it seemed welcoming and secure. It would be our home for the next five days. Annabel looked around and reached out for my hand. She said with a smile, "A front view of you is better than a back view of 'Barney.'" Then she added, "But only slightly."

"That's asinine," I said.

Auntie and Uncle were leaving later in the day. They apologized for their sudden departure and said they had to attend an urgent business meeting in Norwich. I concluded that Auntie had deliberately arranged their three-day absence so that Annabel and I could be together.

On my earlier visit to Fordy I told Auntie of my love for Annabel. She, in turn, spoke to me, at times tearfully, of her lost love, Jack Markham, killed in the trench warfare of World War I. They were engaged to be married.

Jack's death was so devastating that Auntie decided never to marry. Hugh, Jack's younger brother, always attentive and gentlemanly, knew that he could not take his brother's place but three years later he proposed and Auntie accepted.

On the surface the marriage was harmonious but Auntie's continuing grief for her lost Jack shaped the marriage into one of convenience. They never had children.

Mrs. Slack, the housekeeper, showed us to two adjoining bedrooms on the second floor. Both bedrooms had access to a balcony looking across great fields of potatoes and sugar beets, stretching into the distance. The bedrooms were tastefully furnished and shared a sitting area with book-laden shelves, comfortable couches and a fireplace.

After tea we said good-bye to Auntie and Uncle. We embraced and Auntie in an aside said to me, "The house is yours and Annabel's. I want you to enjoy it." Ever after, I suspected a subconscious vicarious motive. Now, twenty-seven years after her loss, she wanted to help two young lovers, caught up in another war.

The car disappeared down the long driveway. Annabel turned to me, "My darling, what bliss. We have three days together."

I replied, "Correction, Miss Lee, we have three days and three nights together."

Before leaving for the evening, Mrs. Slack prepared dinner: roasted chicken with vegetables. We enjoyed this in front of the fire, accompanied by a bottle of prewar French wine, left by Uncle. Jill, Uncle's pet golden retriever, adopted Annabel and made quite a fuss when banished to the scullery for the night.

After dinner we went upstairs. The house alone in its vast fields was in darkness, except for our sitting room. A cold wind from the North sea moaned around the eaves and rustled the leaves in the plum orchard. The ghost of Hereward the Wake, the Anglo-Saxon King, who defended the area from Norman invaders seemed nearby; for Annabel and me, a benign ghost, as nine centuries later we too were Anglo-Saxon defenders against a Continental enemy.

The flat fen land stretched for many miles to the North Sea. When we looked out there was a feeling of space and cold emptiness. We quickly shut the window. The cold outside world with its war could be forgotten for a while. Now alone in a snug room with our love, an enchantment, a spell, enfolded us in a warm embrace.

Annabel had changed into a nightgown covered by a housecoat. She was lovely, her eyes seemed larger in the soft light. We had not been alone since that moonlit night in the field near Albury. Now, the nearby bedrooms with their implication of sleeping together brought a sweet constraint. It was Annabel, with her forthright manner, who came to me. We held each other and kissed. Her lips were soft, her hair fragrant and we stood clasped together, our bodies urgently compliant.

In the early dawn I stirred in my sleep. Recent intimacy had woven a closeness that encompassed sleeping and waking. When I stirred so did Annabel. When I reached out my hand I found hers seeking mine. We drifted on a timeless twilight sea, between sleeping and waking, until the coming light brought us fully awake.

Annabel lay with head on one side, eyes open, lost in thought. I said, "My darling Annabel, where are you, what do you see?"

She turned to me, "I see a day in the future, when this terrible war is over. We are on a beach in Abaco. There is a soft wind in the coconut palms and the air is fragrant with wild geranium. The ocean is calm and gentle waves run softly up the beach. The water is crystal clear and the sand a magical pinky white. Two children, a boy and a girl are shrieking with delight as they play at the water's edge. Their lips are stained purple from ripe seagrapes picked on the dune above."

"The children are beautiful," she said. "A judicious mixture of both our genes."

I said, "Well, they're young and have time to grow out of my contribution."

She gave me a playful slap. "They can never escape the sisal blond hair and long legs," she said.

"And what else do you see?" I asked. She closed her eyes and after a minute said, "We are helping our children build a sand castle. It has a moat, soon filled with water from encroaching waves, until the castle itself is washed away." For some reason, not clear to me until much later, I felt a stab of sadness and looked away.

Annabel reached out, uncovering her breast, and gently turned my face toward hers. "And what do you see in our future?" she asked.

I thought for a minute. "I share with you the dream of playing with our children on a Bahamian beach, but there is a scene that takes precedence."

She asked, "And what is that?"

I brought her nearer to me, our bodies in a close embrace, her lovely face on my chest. "I see two university students on a campus in a northern city. It is spring and the lilacs are blooming. We are hurrying across a campus park. The path winds through ancient oaks under which students sit with their books. We arrive at a lecture hall and take our seats. The English professor, a learned man, but absentminded, arrives late but then fascinates us with his discourse on the music and majesty of the English language. He is an authority on our friend, Chaucer, has mastered Old English pronunciation and quotes from the Canterbury Tales.

> When that April with his shoures soote,
> The droghte of March hath perced to the roote.
> And smale foweles maken melodye
> That slepen al the nyght with open ye.

"We live in a boarding house with other married couples and, when not studying, dream of our life after university. This, of course, includes children, maybe three or four, and beaches and sunshine and always our love for each other."

There were noises from downstairs. In a few minutes Mrs. Slack knocked on the sitting room door and said that she would serve breakfast on the lawn. She had prepared a table in the shelter of a high hedge and we sat facing a warm sun, that promised a beautiful day.

Mrs. Slack offered to drive us to the Sunday service at the little church in Barway. It was a lovely sunny morning and we decided to walk. The path led through open, flat, fertile fields. A few acres of undrained fen provided a habitat for water life, wildfowl and wild flowers. Annabel surprised me with her knowledge of the countryside and pointed out the delicate flowers of cranberry and brilliant yellow bog asphodel. Nearing Barway, long habitation had provided an avenue of elms, a home for rooks and linnets.

Mrs. Slack met us at the church door. She greeted us warmly and led us to a pew near the front. A small brass plaque announced that it was reserved for Squire Markham. The interior of the church was simple and reminded me of St. James Methodist Church in Hope Town.

Mrs. Slack introduced us to the minister, an earnest man of large stature. From his choice of hymns and scripture readings it was apparent that Mrs. Slack had informed him of our naval connection.

The service began with the 1869 hymn, by William Whiting:

> Eternal Father, strong to save,
> Whose arm doth bind the restless wave,
> Who bidd'st the mighty ocean deep
> Its own appointed limits keep;
> O hear us when we cry to thee
> For those in peril on the sea.

The full congregation sang with feeling, the harmonious voices filling the little church. I was content to listen to the sweet soprano of Annabel beside me.

I had been warned by Mrs. Slack and was prepared, when asked by the minister, to read from Psalm 107. Some of the lines were remarkably appropriate and painfully reminiscent of storms at sea.

> They that go down to the sea in ships,
> That do business in great waters;

These see the works of the Lord,
And His wonders in the deep.

For he commandeth,
And raises the stormy wind
Which lifteth up the waves thereof.

They mount up to the heavens,
They go down again to the depths:
Their soul is melted because of trouble.

They reel to and fro,
And stagger like drunken men
And are at their wits end.

When I returned to the pew Annabel whispered to me, somewhat irreverently, "You read so well some of the congregation became sea sick."

It was announced that after the church service a wedding ceremony would take place. Mrs. Slack said that we were invited to stay. Annabel seemed keen, so I agreed.

I was happy that we stayed. The ceremony was simple but touching and soon took on a personal significance. It did not include a sermon but consisted only of vows, prayers and pronouncement.

Mary, the bride, was beautiful, of course. Attended by her bridesmaids she walked slowly up the aisle on the arm of her father and joined James, the groom, standing before the minister.

Annabel and I looked at each other and our thoughts were echoed when the minister announced, "If you are sitting next to your spouse, Mary and James invite you to affirm your vows of commitment by taking hold of the hand of your spouse." I took Annabel's hand and looked into her eyes, now shining with tears.

We followed silently in the commitment: "To hold from this day forward, for better, for worse, for richer, for poorer, in sickness and in health, to love and to cherish, until we are parted by death."

We listened intently to the ceremony of the presentation of the rings, the minister's prayer, a solo sung by the bride's uncle and finally the pronouncement, "What, therefore, God hath joined together, let not man put asunder." When the groom was told to kiss the bride Annabel squeezed my hand. We each knew what the other was thinking.

Outside the church, the congregation dispersed in family groups, in the direction of nearby Barway. Annabel and I set off in the opposite direction, toward Fordy.

Our path led through a green tunnel formed by branches of ancient elms intertwined overhead. The woodland silence was relieved by soft scampering of squirrels and muted cawing of rooks.

At the end of the avenue we sat on a bench looking across a small lake. Waterfowl sat quietly on the surface; they too observing a Sabbath solemnity. Without preamble, I said, "Annabel, I want to marry you, if you'll have me. We'll make our own vows. I wish James and Mary well but no tandem matrimony for us."

Annabel reached for my hand and leaned closer. "Of course, I want to marry you, but when? We're both fighting a war."

"We'll talk," I said, "In the meantime I'd like to speak to Bill and Annie."

She smiled, "You want to ask my father for my hand?"

"I'm new at this," I said, "Isn't that the proper thing to

do?"

We sat for awhile in silence and then, hand in hand, continued on to Fordy. The hedgerows were in bloom and promised an abundance of sloes and blackberries. When nearing the house Jill came bounding to meet us and made the usual fuss over Annabel.

We were happy to remain within the environs of Fordy, picking early blackberries in the nearby hedges or enjoying the stillness within a walled fruit orchard, with its inviting pathways and benches.

The flat fenland gave an uninterrupted view of the horizon. At day's end the western sky became suffused with vibrant light that billowed across the arc of sky in great salmon hued waves, to be gently diluted by approaching darkness until it faded and dissolved. Time seemed to expand as Annabel and I sat on the lawn and rejoiced at this transformation.

Our closeness now intensified and we moved dreamlike through the following days and nights. The calm companionship of day merged swiftly into stormy passion at night, submerging us both, before breaking onto the shores of tenderness.

On our third day I arranged a visit to Wicken Fen, mainly to indulge Annabel's interest in ornithology. Once there I shared her delight.

Wicken Fen is one of the few remaining areas of undrained fen land, a remnant of the strangest of all English landscapes. For centuries a vast area of southeastern England was an inhospitable wilderness of swamps and marshland.

From this half drowned hideaway, Boadicea, in the First Century, and Hereward the Wake, a thousand years later, ventured out to fight against foreign invaders.

Attempts at reclamation in the Middle Ages were accelerated in the seventeenth century when Dutch engineer, Cornelius Vermuyden, introduced - amid fierce local opposition - numerous windmills to drain the Fens.

Annabel and I wandered along wide footpaths through the 730 acres of Wicken Fen, marveling at the rich wildlife. An occasional slight breeze bent the reed tops bringing a whiff of reeds, mud and water mint.

The dykes and reed beds were alive with the chatter of reed warblers and sedge warblers. Annabel pointed out great crested grebes, heron, shoveller and bitterns. I shared her excitement when a pair of bearded tits, lovely in their soft golden colours, made a brief appearance. Annabel said that the sighting of pairs of tits was rare and only in protected country areas. Risking a swift kick on the shins I said, "Not so, there are frequent sightings in London, in the Piccadilly Circus area."

Auntie Grace and Uncle Hugh returned on the fourth day. We left on the following morning. Auntie Grace drove us to the station and came to the platform to see us off. We told her of our commitment to marry. She said, "I'm very happy for both of you." She embraced us both and, with an enigmatic smile said, "I'm not a bit surprised."

CHAPTER 23

Marking Time

As instructed, I returned to Portsmouth Barracks and joined other officers, also awaiting appointments. Most evenings were spent in the bar of the Queens Hotel on the waterfront of nearby Southsea. The first to arrive secured our favourite table looking across to Southsea Parade. From there we observed the posturing of teenage strollers. Gaggles of girls, enacting an age-old courtship ritual, pretended to discourage the attentions of pursuing boys but, by covert over the shoulder glances, ensured that they were followed.

"I remember the ploy well," said one of our group, a teenager himself, just two years before, "don't follow me but I'm going this way."

"And I know which way you went," I said.

The summer was now well advanced. News from the North Atlantic was favourable. After having the upper hand for three and a half years U-boat losses were now more than twice Germany's replacement capacity.

This was an unacceptable situation for the Germans. Admiral Doenitz recalled most of his fleet from the Atlantic. His memoirs reveal that he wrote of this period, "We have lost the Battle of the Atlantic."

It was too late for *HMS Beverley*, 175 other lost warships and 2,452 merchant ships, their hulks scattered across the depths of the wide Atlantic, guarded by ghostly crews. A heavy and tragic cost but not in vain.

The Allies could now, with negligible interference from the U-boats, continue to arm a battered Britain. A flood of food, weapons, raw material and troops from North America poured across the Atlantic. With her allies, Britain was preparing for the final assault on Fortress Europe.

After many months of tense disagreements a plan for landing on the coast of France, in the late spring of 1944, was agreed upon by all the Allies. Known to the planners as Overlord, one of its most important facets was Combined Operations Command, to coordinate sea, air and land forces. Costly lessons had been learned from the calamity of Dieppe and large scale amphibious assaults in Italy and elsewhere. Now, under the inspired leadership of Admiral Louis Mountbatten and his successor, General Laycock, numerous exercises of amphibious operations were conducted with increasing confidence.

I was given overnight liberty and visited Annie and Bill in Albury. We felt incomplete without Annabel, a feeling which intensified as we motored to the Plough in Coldwater for dinner. They knew that I wished to speak of marrying Annabel and made it easier by assuring me at once that the marriage had their blessing.

They convinced me that we should wait until the war ended. With successes in North Africa, the Mediterranean and Russia we were all hopeful that an Allied victory was not far off. In the meantime marriage would interfere with our duties and my impending appointment might be to some distant area far removed from Annabel.

That settled, we toasted the absent Annabel and our eventual marriage. Jack the Stripper was in the room but avoided us. Too bad, I could have told him about the couple in Apalachicola and their pet pig with a wooden leg.

CHAPTER 24

Landing Craft

The day after returning from Albury I was given orders to proceed to a Combined Operations establishment in Scotland. Two days later I arrived in Glasgow and by various buses made my way to the Toward Arms at Toward Point on Loch Ailort.

I was assigned to a comfortable bedroom on the third floor, with a balcony looking down to the shores of the loch. Inviting landscaped terraces ended at the waters edge. A tall flagpole with the white ensign aloft reminded me that I was in a naval establishment.

There was a spacious, comfortable wardroom on the first floor and I discovered a well stocked library on the second floor to which I retreated when time allowed.

I was told that while awaiting appointment to a LCT-Landing Craft Tank - I would with about fifty other Navy and Army officers, take part in a "toughening-up process." Lord Louis Mountbatten had established several such camps in the Clyde area. Most of us had recently arrived and were exposed to horror stories of twenty-mile hikes and early morning swims in the loch followed by runs up Ben-something or other.

Our first trial though, was a thorough medical check-up. We waited stark naked in a shivering queue for inspection by a RN Surgeon Commander. Bearded, sarcastic and with very cold hands he peered into our various apertures, in no particular order. He got his deserts (in a manner of speaking) when he told the poor sod ahead of me to touch his toes. The poor sod's toes, not the Commander's toes. Because of nerves or an unwise diet there was an awesome manifestation of flatulence at the precise moment of inspection. The Surgeon Commander deserves some credit for his forbearance. The "poor sod" was merely sent back to the end of the queue, not back to sea.

Our informants were correct. We were awakened at dawn on the second day and ran up heights so steep that at times we were scrambling upward on all fours. We complained, but having reached the top it all seemed worthwhile. The sun's rays glanced off the mountain peaks and, as we sat and watched, the mist in the valleys became fine spun and wispy and faded away. We lingered long enough to see the leaden surface of the loch far below change subtly to silver.

Later on, we were introduced to "fell running," also known as "point to point." Running in pairs, a precaution against an injured runner lying helpless in the wilderness, we covered about twenty miles through fearsomely rugged countryside. The exact route was left to the devices of each pair of runners: a straight line up and over mountains or a timely circumventing of natural obstacles. A bus at the finish line, with a very patient driver, awaited our arrival. Our supervisors were only mildly interested in our individual times for the run. Their chief concern was the possibility of having to organise a search party. This would make them late for tea.

We were kept busy for several weeks. Most memorable were the combined exercises, employing various types of Landing craft, Army troops and fighter planes.

About three miles down the shores of the loch there was a narrow beach. Landing craft would proceed there and simulate landings. On the way we would be "attacked" by daredevil U. S. Airforce Mustangs and British Spitfires, based at nearby Prestwick.

Several fighters would swoop suddenly through a valley. Descending to wave top height they headed straight for our landing craft, pulling up at the last split second. As they streaked over with just inches to spare there was a crescendo of roaring motors and blank cannon fire. We were happy they were on our side.

At the landing site a well staged enemy defence was enacted with accompanying smoke, gunfire and various explosions. Suppressed laughter from designated "casualties" sometimes marred the intended realism.

With other Naval types I observed the techniques of beaching, disembarking troops and then leaving the beach in a hurry. One thing was certain. I would remember every tiny detail about leaving the beach in a hurry.

During the last three years Britain and the United States continued to build and modify landing craft. The campaigns in Italy and North Africa provided data for continuing improvement and specialization.

By early 1944 they ranged from giant Landing Ships[12] to tiny DUKWs, an amphibious wheeled boat which could drive onto an enemy beach and disappear down the street of any village or town.

We expected to be assigned to LCT Mark 4's (developed by the British through LCT (1) to LCT (3) designs). These Mark 4's were 188 feet long, 39 feet in the beam and capable of carrying six 40-ton or 9 30-ton tanks or 12 loaded 3-ton trucks or 350 tons of cargo, with accompanying troops. The Mark 4's crew was usually 2 officers and 12 men.

---

[12] Landing Ships: Up to 500 feet in length; tonnage: over 14,500 tons.

CHAPTER 25

New Year's Eve - 1944

The eve of New Years was of special significance in Scotland, combining ceremony and gaiety and taking precedence over Christmas. In some areas First Footing still took place. This ancient ritual was meant to keep at bay evil spirits and hostile forces during the coming year.

For us at the Toward Arms the celebrations were simplified. There was an abundance of whiskey, with many toasts for victory in the new year and, at midnight, repeated singing of Robert Burn's Auld Lang Syne. It was all very noisy with people in various stages of drunkenness from jocose and verbose to lachrymose and comatose.

I left early and was in bed by 0200 and awoke at 0700. I wanted to get a letter on its way to Annabel.

New Years morning - 1944

My darling Annabel,

I'm in my favourite chair in a bay window in the library looking across the silver-gray surface of the loch. The mountains beyond are wraithlike through shifting dark clouds. I miss you this New Year's morning, hopefully the last we'll be apart. There was a party last night, of course, with lots of shouting and toasting of good news from the war front and many toasts for victory in the new year.

You were in my thoughts every minute. Where were you? Did you think of me also? Did my love reach you across these wild uplands and the valleys and dales of England? Did you feel my kiss at midnight? I reach out now and touch you, my lover, my friend, and remind you that we'll be together for all the New Years yet to come.

Bill and Annie will have told you of my visit to Albury. They made it easy for me. My appointment to this "far northern outpost" supports their reasoning that our marriage should wait until the war is over.

I have to confess that since we were together at Fordy I feel more vulnerable. Before then I faced the dangers of war with a certain brashness, lulled into imprudence by a feeling of youthful invulnerability. Now, I want desperately to stay alive, to be with you. I'm not likely to be tested soon as there are few enemy planes or craft in this somewhat protected area.

While writing, the clouds have vanished, the mountains are clearly defined and the surface of the loch sparkles with golden light, the promise of a bright new year. Take care of yourself my darling Annabel. And now you are kissed farewell.

Chester

P.S. I leave tomorrow to join a Landing Craft Mark 4 LCT 801, as second in command.

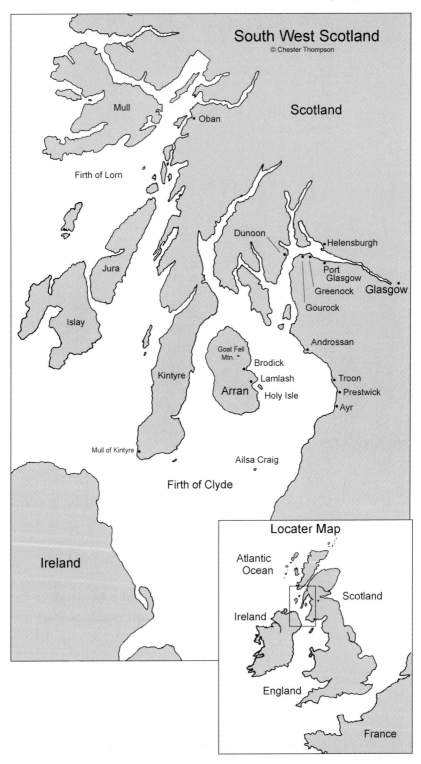

South West Scotland
© Chester Thompson

Scotland

Mull

Oban

Firth of Lorn

Dunoon

Helensburgh

Port Glasgow

Greenock

Glasgow

Gourock

Jura

Androssan

Islay

Goat Fell Mtn.

Brodick

Kintyre

Lamlash

Troon

Arran

Prestwick

Holy Isle

Ayr

Mull of Kintyre

Ailsa Craig

Firth of Clyde

Ireland

Locater Map

Atlantic Ocean

Scotland

Ireland

England

France

CHAPTER 26

LCT 801

On arrival in Port Glasgow, I proceeded to Lamonts Shipyard, an enclosed cluttered area on the south bank of the river Clyde. Several LCT Mark 4's were tied alongside but no sign of LCT 801.

Mr. Gaul, the yard foreman, came to my rescue. He led me through a maze of various craft under repair in the dry dock area. Pausing, he pointed to one with 801 barely discernible on the bow.

I gazed with dismay at the bottom of what appeared to be an enormous sardine tin resting on steel girders about 8 feet above the ground. Tall ladders alongside gave access to the deck above.

Noting my distress Mr. Gaul said, "Aye, She'll be a great wee craft when we get her in't sea." I'd never seen anything less feminine, on the bottom or elsewhere, and wondered how I could ever bring myself to call it "she."

Mr. Gaul led me to his office and gave me a restorative tot of whiskey. I must have still looked pale and we had another "wee drop." He explained that, in company with another LCT, *801* had been driven ashore, in a freak storm, off Strone Point in Holy Loch. He expected repairs to be completed by January 16th.

Sucking affectionately at an unlit pipe Mr. Gaul ended every sentence with a ruminative "Aye." We immediately became good friends and I saw him often while awaiting the return of my Commanding Officer and the crew. He served in WWI as a Sergeant Major in the Cameron Highlanders and had many stories to tell of forced marches and life in the trenches.

I found accommodation in the Business Men's Club in Glasgow an easy commute to Lamonts Ship Yard. There was lots of time to look around the second largest city in the British Empire, as was claimed in the Victorian era. Its earliest history is shrouded in myth, its name deriving from the Celtic Glas-cu, meaning "the dear green place," a far cry from the inebriate and grimy image now sometimes unkindly bestowed.

Sprawling amidst steep hills the city spreads out on both banks of the river Clyde. I walked along the north bank and up the appropriately named High Street to Glasgow Cathedral. Built in 1136, it is dedicated to St. Mungo, the city's patron saint. Steps lead from the upper church with its lofty nave and stained glass windows to the lower church. I walked in a dim light and admired what is said to be the most glorious example of medieval architecture in Scotland. Immense stone columns support delicate fan vaulting, looking ethereal in the half-light. The tomb of St. Mungo is the centrepiece.

As promised by Mr. Gaul, *LCT 801* was launched on the afternoon of January 16th and was immediately transformed from dirty slabs of metal into a ship. Our generator purred away. The wash from passing ships rocked us gently. I decided that, after all, she was a "she." Not a lovely lady but, with her new paint job and the dockyard grime washed off, she was pretty and dependable.

Our sailing for Troon was delayed until the morning of January 20th. Mr. Gaul came to the dockside to see us off. I gave him a farewell present: a new pipe, a pound of the best tobacco and a box of matches.

Harvey 'Nick' Nicholson, my Commanding Officer, was just a few months my senior. Though quite different we soon became good friends. I was talkative, Nick a man of few words. One day when catching a bus in Glasgow for Port Glasgow a young lady boarded just ahead of us. I said to Nick that she was remarkably well endowed, or words to that effect. We found seats and were silent throughout the journey. When leaving the bus thirty minutes later Nick said, to my momentary puzzlement, "Yes, she is."

Living in the close quarters of an *LCT* required some adjustments. Differences were resolved in a good-natured manner. The nearest to a reprimand occurred during a period when we were idle for a few days, awaiting orders.

Ship's routine was relaxed and Nick quite deservedly, was able to sleep in, to arise at 10 00 for late breakfast served by Steward Hobson. By long habit I arose early to enjoy the morning, sometimes singing and whistling as I went about my various tasks. I awoke one morning to find a Notice, affixed to my cabin door, half in jest but unmistakably firm.

"NOTICE"
Attention: First Lieutenant
Chester Thompson
All whistling, singing, shouting and other forms of merriment are strictly forbidden before 10 00 hours.
Sub Lieutenant Harvey Nicholson
Commanding Officer
LCT 801

CHAPTER 27

A Stormy Odyssey

We set off from Port Glasgow, our new ensign proudly flying. It would take several days to go thirty miles.

Excerpts from my diary remind me vividly of that stormy odyssey.

Thursday, January 20th

As we set off, Mr. Gaul and his workmen came to have a final look at the object of their last month's work. The pounding of the motors, the beginning of a new voyage, was exciting. On the move again!

We are at anchor for the night in the shelter of nearby Holy Loch, as we are to be boarded tomorrow by the Compass Swinging Officer, a necessary procedure to adjust the compasses to changes in the ship's magnetism while on dry dock.

The sky is dark and wind and rain make for a gloomy evening. The generator will be turned off at 22 30 hours but for now it is warm and cosy inside.

Friday, 21st

This morning we moved around Greenock

Bay for three hours while the compasses were adjusted. After that, with many delays, we refueled from the tanker *Juliana*.

It has been stormy all day and after several attempts we were unable to secure to a buoy so we anchored in seven fathoms. The wind increases in volume and roars around the superstructure - there is a storm brewing. No doubt we're in for a restless night, but the day was a lot of fun.

Saturday, 22nd

I went on the bridge at 04 00 with O/Sea Hull. It was cold with a stinging wind whirling the snow around. The storm increased in violence. I feared that we would drag the anchor and made plans accordingly. It abated at about 05 30 and I sent Hull to the galley to make coffee. Very welcome it was too.

Hull and I crouched, heads bowed, away from the sting of driving snow and sleet. Hull was curious about Bahamian hurricanes and I spoke of ones I'd been through.

Nick relieved me at 06 15 and I was happy to get in bed. Back on the bridge at 08 00. At 08 45 we saw through driving rain and sleet that the signal light at Princes Pier was wearily signaling: ●—●● —●—● — (LCT). We acknowledged and got "who R U?" When told, they signaled, "Sailing instructions cancelled until weather moderates." So we're still at anchor - our supply of bread is almost gone - one slice per man at tea time.

Sunday, 23rd

We were ready to proceed this morning but got a Negative to our "Request to proceed." The hills are white with snow and a chill wind blows. The gannets are restless, swooping around and shrieking, "No bread sur." How well I know, having had cake only for tea.

Monday, 24th

Again this morning we signaled for permission to sail but were told, "Sailing cancelled." Fortunately they granted our request for a boat. We now have bread, potatoes, and as a Sunday treat, 12 oranges. Mine is lying on the sideboard, a tempting golden ball, for later.

Today the coxs'n reported O/Sea Hull for using obscene language. Secretly I sympathize; he is young, life is hard. I'll have a private talk with him, hopefully without having to resort to obscene language!

Tuesday, 25th

At 03 00 I was awakened by the pounding of the engines. Dressing hurriedly I battled my way to the bridge, occupied by a shivering Nick. A storm was raging, the anchor dragging.

It was very cold and dark and driving rain and sleet made the taking of bearings very difficult. Nick was persistent and took bearings every few minutes. I supplied him with hot coffee and cigarettes which I lit in the shelter of the wheelhouse. I had all hands awakened and standing by.

At 04 00 we were narrowly missed by LCT 797 which had broken away and was steaming around the bay. Our men were quite cheerful and it was good to hear occasional laughter in the darkness.

Daylight revealed that we had dragged to within 4 cables[13] of the shore. The storm had now decreased. At 10 00 Nick went below for some sleep. At 11 00 we were dragging again so I ordered that the anchor be taken in, requiring the aid of full astern to do so; as of course, we're anchored by the stern.

As we passed LCT 797 I gave him a cheery "Good morning" to which he responded, "What a nerve!"

We inched our way up the bay for about 6 cables and dropped anchor. It failed to hold. We dragged a hundred yards in about 15 minutes. I tried again and we dragged. After the third try I decided to steam around until the wind decreased.

Nick relieved me at 14 30. I went to bed for an hour. At 17 00 the weather had improved and we anchored. I was early in bed and slept soundly, all night.

Wednesday, 26th

I awoke refreshed and Hobson served a breakfast of bacon and powdered egg omelet. 09 30 up anchor. 14 00 arrived off Ardrossan, sailed up and down off the signal station until told to proceed to Brodick Bay, on the Isle of Arran. We left at 15 30 to make the crossing and arrived at 17 30. As expected the crossing was rough. Some of the crew were sea

---

[13] Cable: In the Royal Navy equal to 100 fathoms or one-tenth of a sea mile (approximately 200 yards or 185 metres).

sick and lay around like dead flies.

Thursday, 27th

The weather got much worse during the night but we were anchored securely about 10 cables from the shore. LCT 797 and 956 made it across as well and are safely at anchor nearby. Having gone through the storms together I'm anxious to meet their crews. Nick showed his skill at carpentry today and made a duckboard for the wardroom entrance.

This afternoon 3 aircraft carriers anchored nearby. We watched with envy as a hockey game was played on the flight deck of the nearest.

Brodick Bay is a small jumble of houses, with cultivated fields behind, in the shadow of great hills dominated by 2,800 feet Goat Fell. Nick pointed out a yellow curving sandy beach which, he says, provides good bathing in the summer. Not for me. Even in Bahamas I only swim between May and October, unless spear-fishing for a meal.

Friday, 28th

A calm morning but with spitting rain. We left Brodick at 09 15, ahead of LCT 797 and 956. Off Ardrossan by 11 00 and boarded by a Gunnery Officer. All went well. The first time I've seen the PAC's fired. Quite a novel sight, as the parachutes opened at 1,000 feet. Supposed to be very effective at snagging attacking enemy aircraft.

Gunnery trials over we sailed for Troon and arrived off shore at 13 15. It had taken sev-

en days to cover the thirty miles from Port
Glasgow. Not a promising beginning for the
trials ahead. The harbour is quite confined,
collisions and jetty-bashing frequent. The entrance is just 60 feet in width. Nick made a
splendid job of bringing us alongside.

CHAPTER 28

Getting Ready

On arrival off Troon we stood by until a line of fluttering flags indicated permission to enter. Troon harbour is notoriously difficult to negotiate. I had the crew stand by with fenders, a seamanlike precaution and no reflection on Nick's ship handling skills.

The entrance is sixty feet wide, giving us clearance of just ten feet on each side. Nick handled it masterfully and we were soon tied alongside another craft. With the engines now shut down we felt great relief. Our interminable stormy seven-day voyage was finally over.

The Clyde area, with Troon as headquarters, was an important centre for the organization and practice of amphibious operations. A stream of new landing craft, their manning and training of crews would test the resources of the area Combined Operations Command.

Nearby Prestwick airfield provided units from the Royal Air Force and U.S. Air Force. Army troops and vehicles were from Army groups in the area.

With the increasing activity, Troon harbour was woefully inadequate. The inexperience of many ship handlers resulted in frequent collisions and jetty-bashings.

LCT 956 and *797* arrived in the late afternoon and tied up nearby. Nick knew Geoffrey Trevor, the CO of *956*, a two striper who had seen service in the Mediterranean. We were to benefit from his freely given counsel. His First Lieutenant, Australian Bill Marlow, became my chum and later we were together in the Commanding Officers course.

They came aboard 801 at sundown, with Robert Davenport and George Edgar, CO and First Lieutenant of 797. We had an amusing time comparing notes on our voyage from Port Glasgow. They were to be entertaining and cooperative companions.

George Edgar the First Lieutenant of 797 became quite tiddly and told his version of the storm in Greenock Bay, looking pleased when I said, "Yes, you missed us by three feet."

During the next few weeks, whenever we met, George invariably told his storm story, always asking me to verify the wind force, now increased in the telling to hurricane strength.

When our guests left Nick and I rushed ashore to enjoy our first showers in ten days. The crew had already indulged and at evening rounds we were all unusually clean and fragrant. I told the crew that for the next two weeks our craft and crew would be undergoing a series of inspections. I explained to the best of my knowledge what was expected of all crewmembers.

Next morning the craft swarmed with inspecting officials: kit musters for the ratings and medical and dental inspections for everyone.

This was followed by an address from Captain Stanford RN, Commanding Officer, Major Landing Craft, attended by the crews of *LCT* 801, 956, 797 and others.

The Captain spoke of the "Big Landing" as if it was imminent. "We're just waiting for good weather," he said.

We were all very attentive as he spoke of the urgency of the situation. When he ended with a dramatic, "Good luck to you all," we were all ready to write our last wills.

The next day we listened to a gruesome lecture by a medical officer who spoke casually of the correct first aid to a limbless torso. He did not explain first aid procedures for a headless torso.

Over the next few days lectures on shore alternated with exercises at sea, if the weather was suitable.

The weather was quite unsuitable on the day chosen to exercise "Repel Boarders." We were no sooner out of the harbour when some of the crew became seasick. They managed though and the enactment was quite realistic. A B Halstead ran stooping to the shelter of the ramp door, armed with a Lanchester. From there he opened fire on an imaginary E-boat attempting to come alongside. We pretended to help with the 20mm cannon even though the angle of bearing was not right. Halstead was smiling broadly but hopefully he'll never be exposed to the real thing.

Due to unpredictable ship movements receiving mail was always haphazard. While in Troon I received a batch of 12 letters and four parcels, the first in a month. I found a quiet place to read the welcome letters from my mother, sister, and other family members in Nassau.

Included was a letter from dear Aunt Emmie. She reminded me to always be a good boy. Her concern for my morals was stronger than her spelling skills. She warned me not to have any bed companions.

There was a long awaited letter from Annabel.

My darling Chester,

You seem so far away. Your New Years letter took weeks to arrive and that was a month ago. I'm lonely and miss you all the time. I hope you haven't met some pretty Scots lassie!

I'm to be sent to another place and will be stationed near Dad's good friend, Dr. Duff. You will remember that Dad gave you his address and phone number. Please direct your letters there.

I've changed my mind about marriage. I don't think we should wait until the war is over. Women are allowed to change their minds!

Marriage will celebrate how precious we are to each other. It need not interfere with our duties. It could even help, a salve to ease this dreadful loneliness when we're apart.

I'm to be given a weeks leave before my new posting and will go to Albury to be with Mom and Dad. I believe they'll understand how I feel about marriage. You will not have to go on your knees to Bill again!

I have a good idea of what you're going through and understand that you cannot join me in Albury. There is a feeling of urgency abroad, although we don't speak about it.

I read the letter several times. Images of Annabel as a teenager mingled with the profound closeness we now shared as adults. I now agreed with her that our marriage be sooner rather than an indefinite wait for war's end. I had no doubt that she would get Bill and Annie's blessing.

CHAPTER 29

Dawn Landings

The small neat town of Troon meandered along the Ayrshire coast, a stark contrast to the congestion and grime of industrial Port Glasgow, Gourock and Helensborough. A promenade hugged the shoreline, a delightful walkway at days end, with a view to the west.

A popular watering hole, the centrally located Marine Hotel was also the venue for various training courses. It was here that prospective *LCT* commanding officers were sent for certification.

Troon was our base for three or four weeks. The crew attended lectures and workshops in their specialties. Nick and I often looked in on the crew when not attending other lectures. The always cheerful Hobson, our Cook/Steward, attended a workshop, with no obvious improvement.

One afternoon the crews of *LCT* 801, 797 and 956 were taken by bus to Prestwick Airport, a few miles south of Troon. We were familiar with the swift Spitfires and Mustangs. It was comforting to see many other aircraft for our protection when landing on enemy beaches. I had a good look at Lancasters, one of which was being flown by brother Leonard on bombing raids over Germany, from a base in Yorkshire.

In suitable weather various exercises took place at sea. Without notice one morning, Squadron Commander Richard Moir came on board. Known as "Deadeye Dick" it was said that his keen eye could see around corners.

Firstly, there was to be an inspection of the craft. While Nick kept the Commander occupied on the bridge I scurried around to check that all was in order.

In particular, I tried to hide a wheelbarrow we had "won," with the connivance of the kind Mr. Gaul, when leaving Lamonts Shipyard. It was now used frequently for trundling items around the tank deck. Wheelbarrows were not part of ships stores and if seen would attract adverse comment from the alert Commander. I quickly covered it with a piece of cargo netting.

Inspection over, the Commander ordered that we proceed to sea. Away from traffic to and from Troon and under the vigilant eye of the Commander we exercised "Action," during which Nick was "wounded" and Leading Seaman Watts "killed."

I took over on the bridge, the Coxs'n took charge of the gun's crew and Ordinary Seaman Sturdy was at the steering wheel. The "wounded" Nick signaled to me frantically, behind the Commander's back, to ensure that I was on the right course.

The Commander seemed quite pleased. When we saw him off at the pier he indicated that I should walk with him for a few steps. He said to me, with a smile, "I see, First Lieutenant, that you 'won' a wheelbarrow. Very useful I'm sure. Maybe all *LCTs* should have one?"

"Yes Sir," I said, as I saluted and returned aboard.

On another day with the sky cloudless, the sun warm and not a ripple on the surface we went to sea, in company with two other, *LCTs*, for a "Shoot." We steamed around about three cables from a floating box and most of the crew took turns on the 20mm Oerlikon. When the target was finally hit there was an involuntary response from the gunner, "Take that, you f----r."

An aircraft came by towing a drogue, which was promptly shot down by our gun's crew. (The drogue was shot down not the aircraft!) It was also claimed by *LCT 797*, starting a week long controversy.

In due course our flotilla was sent to Lamlash on the Isle of Arran. Shaped like a kidney bean, Arran is twenty miles in length, its northern half mountainous with 2866 feet Goat Fell dominating several other peaks. Its southern half is lower with a milder climate.

Legend has it that Robert Bruce, before freeing Scotland from English rule by winning the Battle of Bannockburn in 1314, found refuge in a cave on Arran. There, when all seemed lost, he found hope and patience by watching a spider perseveringly spin its web. It was from Arran that he saw a beacon on the Ayrshire coast, signaling him to cross and fight for his crown.

Lamlash harbour has a muddy bottom with poor anchorage. A number of buoys, each capable of holding three *LCTs,* provide secure berths. Often, heavy winds blew down from the hills and picking up the buoy could take more than one attempt.

Lamlash, with Brodick Bay just three miles north, became quite familiar. The focus of our existence and months of training was that sooner or later we would land troops and vehicles on enemy beaches. So now, in these peaceful waters we perfected our skills in beaching.

The usual procedure was to leave Lamlash just after midnight and rendezvous in the waters just east of Arran. In coordination with Army and Air force units a landing at dawn would take place on the beaches of Brodick Bay.

On board the *LCTs* the beaching process began with driving the craft very slowly on to the shore and dropping the stern anchor about fifty yards from the beach. As the bow of the craft slid on to the beach the ramp was lowered. Vehicles with accompanying troops then drove off the craft.

There is a danger that the craft might slide off the beach before unloading is completed. Therefore, the motors are kept running with the CO on the bridge and engine room staff at their stations. The First Lieutenant stands near the ramp giving manual signals to the CO, if necessary. With an ebb tide there is a danger of getting stuck on the beach and having to wait until the tide turns again.

The stern anchor can prevent the stern from slewing on to the beach. Its main function however, is to assist in pulling the craft off the beach. The wire cable, to which the anchor is attached, is wound around the capstan and drawn in by an auxiliary engine.

Our connection to the village of Lamlash was a trot-boat that, in good weather, made a scheduled tour of the harbour. For our entertainment the good citizens of Lamlash provided a weekly program of dances on three nights and a cinema showing on another three nights.

A circular to the *LCTs* intriguingly announced that the ladies of the Church of Scotland offered hot baths to naval personnel. Nick said that he was quite capable of bathing by himself.

Nick and I ventured ashore one night with two companions and taxied to the Douglas Hotel in Brodick Bay. After a bibulous dinner we decided to walk the three miles back to Lamlash, across heather covered hills. The moon was full and the walk enjoyable until Nick decided that he could outrun a rabbit that leaped up in our path.

Protected by the immunity of the intoxicated, he survived several somersaults and downhill slides with only minor scratches. All of us, including Nick – and the rabbit – thought it highly hilarious and fell about with laughter. We caught the last trot-boat and after a cold hour long tour of the harbour arrived on board sober and ready for bed.

CHAPTER 30

Ailsa Craig

There were recurrent rumours that our Flotilla would soon be heading for Southampton. But weeks went by and our beaching exercises continued. Often, in miserable weather, we slipped from our buoys at midnight and milled around in intense darkness east of Lamlash. With navigation lights of the other craft barely visible a lot of signalling went on until all twelve ships of our flotilla were in place. We then proceeded to a dawn landing at Brodick Bay.

So that we would be exposed to a longer voyage before beaching we sometimes left Lamlash in the early evening. When formed up we steamed south about twenty miles, around the jagged cliffs of Ailsa Craig and then north to Brodick Bay.

On these occasions we were usually back in Lamlash by mid morning, in time to catch up on lost sleep.

In the middle of the Firth of Clyde, about ten miles off the Ayrshire coast, Ailsa Craig (Fairy Rock, in Gaelic) is ¾ mile long and ½ mile wide, with an elevation of 1114 feet. From its summit on a clear day one can see for thirty miles.

Halfway between Glasgow in Scotland and Belfast in Northern Ireland Ailsa Craig is nicknamed Paddy's Milestone.

One day, detached from the flotilla, we were on gunnery practice in the area near Ailsa Craig. I persuaded Nick to let me land. It was a clear sunny day and I clambered to the top amidst a cacophony of shrieks from nesting gannets. Great blue and green distances spread before me and I seemed on top of the world.

Twenty miles to the north, on the Isle of Arran, Goat Fell at 2866 feet could be clearly seen. The coast of Ayrshire, Holy Isle and Pladda Isle all seemed quite near.

A flotilla of *LCTs* off the Ayrshire coast were tiny beetles on the sea's flat surface.

A feeling of detachment was evoked which quickly vanished as, picking my way down the grassy slopes, I encountered a billy goat that stood its ground with a "don't mess with me" look. I gave him a wide berth and scurried down to my waiting craft.

LCT Mark 4's in line ahead.

CHAPTER 31

Farewell to LCT 801

Many weeks had passed since captain Stanford spoke of the Big Landing. Now an increasing movement of landing craft to the South indicated that, at least the Allies were assembling at the starting line.

We were weary of continuing rumours but one day in early April all the C.O.'s of our Flotilla were summoned to a meeting in Troon. When Nick returned he asked me to go to his cabin. "We're going South," he said. Then, with some hesitation, "but not you Tommy, you'll be in the next Commanding Officers course, your relief will join us in Oban."

I was silent. Our friendship had deepened in the last weeks, and I ventured, "I believe you've arranged my departure so that I might miss the Big Landing."

"Not so," he said, "you've been in line for command since the day you joined 801. Lt. Cdr. Moir has now made it happen. Bill Marlow from 956 will be taking the course with you."

The next day we left for Oban at 15 00 hours and immediately ran into a storm, with snow driven parallel to the waves. It was the Firth of Clyde's way of saying farewell and was of short duration.

We were rewarded with a blazing sunset as we approached the Mull of Kintyre. This is the nearest Britain gets to Ireland. Paddy from the engine room came on deck and looked longingly at his homeland, just twelve miles away.

The bulbous South end of Kintyre has some spectacular hill views, now shadowy with approaching darkness. When west of Kintyre we altered course to the North. I had the midnight watch and a spitting rain sometimes blanked out the tiny blue stern light of the craft ahead.

I was up early the following morning as I did not want to miss the approach to Oban. The small town has a superb setting with the island of Kerrery providing a natural shelter.

We were secured to a berth by 10 30 hours and at 14 00 hours Sub. Lieutenant Geoffrey Smale, my relief, came onboard. We spent the afternoon together while I turned over my logs and the ship's accounts.

Geoff and I became instant friends and later I was a guest at his home in the countryside near Exeter. His mother was determined to fatten me during a long weekend. On politely refusing third helpings she would implore, "Oh you must have it, Tommy, or my feelings will be hurt."

The next morning in Oban was "out hanky" time. All the crew were on deck to say "Cheerio." The coxs'n said, "We'll take good care of your wheelbarrow."

Nick said, "All the best Tommy and I hope you get a good one." We'd already agreed that, when the war was over, we'd have a reunion in New Zealand. Fate would arrange a meeting sooner, during the war, when our two craft were sent on a special assignment.

I returned to Troon the next day and checked in at the Marine Hotel, venue for the C.O.'s course. We were kept busy for the next ten days. The lectures and exercises in Coastal Navigation were useful. Otherwise, there was repetition of material.

Fortunately the weather was kind and we were at sea for four days for exercises as a flotilla. It would be assumed that the Flotilla Leader was "killed" and his craft damaged by enemy action. We then took turns being in command of the Flotilla, a likely scenario when proceeding to a landing on an enemy beach.

We were also lectured on procedures when detached from a flotilla. We were to discover that in practice we often sailed alone or in groupings of less than twelve. Usually, the senior officer (in terms of date of being commissioned) was in command, although circumstances often dictated otherwise.

On our last day some of us were informed of our appointments. I had a pleasant meeting with Lt. Cdr. Moir, who avoided the subject of wheelbarrows. He told me that I would be going to Grimsby to take command of *LCT 527*. "This is one of the early Mark 4's," he said, "and has seen service in the Mediterranean."

He explained that the craft was on dry dock undergoing repairs, with launching in about three weeks. It was reminiscent of being sent to the dry docked *LCT 801* in Port Glasgow.

However, there was a dimension to this situation that filled me with joy; once again Lady Luck was smiling on me. I remembered the words of brother Maurice, now on a battleship in the Far East, "Chester, you're the luckiest man I know."

Annabel was now a Wren instructor in Hull, not far from Grimsby. I telephoned our friend, Dr. Duff, in Grimsby and spoke to his wife Kathleen. She promised to let Annabel know that I was on my way to Grimsby and would be in the area for two or three weeks.

...to be continued.

ChesterThompson - 1945
Lieutenant RNVR

The Long Day Wanes ...

A Memoir of Love and War

Part Two

ACKNOWLEDGEMENT

Among the many people to whom I am indebted I must mention those readers of Part One—they will know who they are—who gently reminded me that Part Two was overdue.

Thanks are due to Sharon Albury—daughter of my friend Harrington Albury, Royal Navy wartime submariner—who, with wit and perception, transformed my illegible scrawl into a neat manuscript.

The final collating of manuscript, photos, maps and other manifold details of publishing was skillfully provided by Steve Dodge of White Sound Press, assisted by Marjorie Dodge and Jamie Gutierrez Dodge. I am grateful.

My wife Joan and daughters Juliana and Christina were always supportive. Throughout the writing process I was motivated in large measure to provide a glimpse into the past for my grandchildren: Juliana, Alexandra, Jessica, Graham, Sarah, Thomas, Andrew, Anna, Michael, Laura, Sean—and their children.

Autobiography can be the laying to rest of ghosts as well as an ordering of the mind.

A day unremembered is like a soul not born. What indeed was that summer if not re-called? That voyage? That act of love?

So any bits of warm life preserved by the pen are trophies snatched from the dark, are branches of leaves fished out of the flood, are tiny arrests of mortality.

Laurie Lee

The Long Day Wanes, part II, is a sequel to the first book of the same name, dedicated to Bahamian servicemen who died in World War II. It is the story of long, stormy days and nights ferrying vehicles or other cargo across the English Channel to the beaches of Normandy for the Allies' final push into Germany.

This is the story of the author, a young Bahamian from Abaco, who as commander of the LCT 527 played his part in the "Big Landing." It is a story of love, of death, of deprivation, of tense nerves, sleepless nights and a broken heart, but in the end – victory. It is a story, touchingly told, of the struggle to turn the lights "on again, all over the world"

Eileen Carron, Editor/Publisher,
The Tribune

TABLE OF CONTENTS

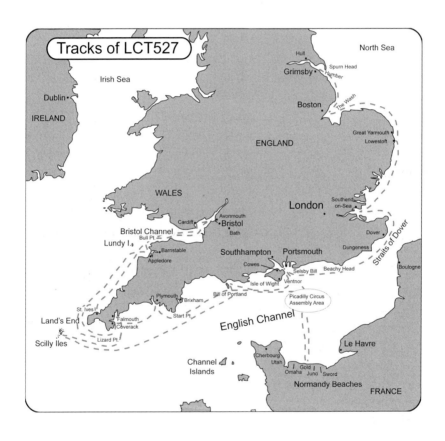

FOREWORD

From the mountaintop of the present we can trace the climactic clash of arms that began on the Normandy beaches in June of 1944 and ended with an Allied victory in Europe in May of 1945. However, in the spring of 1944, history could have gone off in other directions.

In early 1944 a ruthless Hitler was still master of Europe. A battered but defiant Britain had survived the evacuation from Dunkirk, a threatened German invasion, the disastrous Dieppe Raid, the carnage of bombing raids and the close run Battle of the Atlantic. Now, aided by North America, an attack on Fortress Europe could no longer be delayed.

During the months leading up to the Big Landing (as we then knew it) many soldiers and sailors, though superbly trained, viewed the future with foreboding.

We could not forget the retreat from Dunkirk, the slaughter on the beaches of Dieppe and the murderous battles at Anzio. Our mission was now a seemingly do-or-die landing on the French coast, guarded by a formidable foe with his back to the wall.

It was evident from increasing numbers of landing craft heading south that the Big Landing was imminent. Unknown to us at the time was the enormity of the concentration of troops and materials, brought from elsewhere in Britain and from North America, waiting near embarkation points. Churchill wrote in his memoirs:

All southern England became a vast military camp, filled with men trained to come to grips with the Germans across the waters.

Max Hastings, scholar and historian, in his masterly work *Overlord*, writes:

> By the spring of 1944, all of southern England and much of the rest of the country had become a vast military encampment. Under the trees beside the roads, protected by corrugated iron, stood dump after dump of artillery ammunition, mines, engineering stores, pierced plank and wire. The soldiers themselves were awed by the tank and vehicle parks in the fields, where Sherman tanks and jeeps, Dodge trucks and artillery pieces stood in ranks reaching to the horizon. Above all, there were the men – 20 American divisions,[1] 14 British, three Canadian, one French, one Polish, and hundreds of thousands of special forces, corps troops, headquarters units, lines of communication personnel. They were packed into Nissen and Quonset huts, tents and requisitioned country houses from Cornwall to Kent and far northwards up the length of the country. Some were homesick, some excited, a few eager to find any means of escape from the terrifying venture in front of them. Most were impatient to end the months or years of training and to begin this thing upon which all their thoughts had been focused for so long.

---

[1] A division consisted of 15,000 to 20,000 men.

Nearly three million Allied solders, sailors and airmen were ready for the assault. The Supreme Commander, General Eisenhower, recalled:

> The mighty host was as tense as a coiled spring and indeed that is exactly what it was – coiled for the moment when its energy should be released to vault the English Channel in the greatest amphibious assault ever attempted.

In retrospect it seems miraculous that this unprecedented movement of troops escaped the attention of the Germans. The answer is summed up in Churchill's classic remark made at a planning conference, "In wartime truth is so precious she should always be attended by a bodyguard of lies."

The Allies deceived Hitler by various stratagems. For example, a ghost army, known as FUSAG (First United States Army Group), complete with fake equipment, was planted in Southeastern England so that Hitler would believe a landing was intended at Pas-de-Calais, the nearest point in France to England. Hopefully any hint of a landing in Normandy or elsewhere might be considered a diversion from this fictitious "main thrust" at Pas-de-Calais.

This deceit was supported by "leaking" various bits of misinformation which, when assembled by Hitler's Intelligence, further puzzled the enemy as to the Allies' intentions.

Helpful too was a continuing campaign to make civilians and the armed services more aware of the importance of secrecy. Signs were displayed in public areas: "Walls have ears" and "If you tell <u>ANYONE</u> it is no longer a secret."

The security campaign seemed to work. Long after the War I met Maurice East[2], a RCAF pilot who had been stationed at Church Lawford in Warwickshire. He fell in love with a Wren stationed at Gayhurst Manor in Buckinghamshire. The attraction was mutual, an affaire d'amour ensued, with many opportunities for pillow talk. Over thirty years later, in 1976, on the publication of *Bodyguard of Lies* by Anthony Cave Brown, the RCAF officer discovered that Gayhurst Manor had been an outstation of Bletchley Park, the headquarters of ULTRA, history's most secret code-breaking organization. To his utter astonishment, he realized that his former lover had been a covert participant in that remarkable episode. He also realized why, having flown over Gayhurst Manor to dip his plane's wings to his beloved, he was court-martialed. He barely escaped conviction.

These were the situations and events to which I would be exposed as, on a sunny day in May 1944, I walked to the Troon train station to begin my journey to Grimsby. Foremost in my thoughts was being with Annabel Lee, now at a WRNS[3] establishment in Hull near Grimsby.

---

[2]Maurice East was born in England and raised and educated in the United States. He joined the Royal Canadian Air Force in 1942, graduated as a pilot and spent two years based in England in Bomber Command. After a stint as a Regular Officer in the post-war Air Force, he embarked on a career in the tourist industry and now owns and operates Killarney Mountain Lodge, a popular adventure resort in Killarney, Ontario, Canada.

[3]Women's Royal Naval Service; members were known as Wrens.

Chapter 1

HIS MAJESTY'S LCT 527

A bombing raid on nearby Hull delayed our arrival in Grimsby for several hours. Fearful of Grimsby being also targeted it was thought prudent to halt our train in the countryside near the industrial town of Scunthorpe.

With the engine silent we sat like a ship becalmed on a darkened ocean, an impression heightened by firefly flashes from the direction of Hull. My thoughts were of Annabel in Hull. I could only hope that she was in a safe place.

An interminable delay was borne with that characteristic British talent for waiting it out. In our darkened carriage good natured bantering relieved the tedium; there was more laughter than moaning.

A young lady, seated precariously between two sailors (I was not one of them), brought roars of laughter when she shouted into the darkness, "Take your hand off my knee!" "No not you!" "You!" I've never been certain if the remark was entirely in jest.

It was after midnight when we clattered into Grimsby station. The town and docks had been spared but fifteen miles away the docks of Hull had been targeted.

I checked my luggage at the station and found my way through the unlit and almost deserted streets to the nearby Royal Hotel, the few people about hurrying ghostlike through the darkness.

The glow of fires from the direction of Hull and nearby Immingham was sombre indication of bomb damage, the far-off wail of ambulances and fire engines an ominous hint of casualties.

A sleepy clerk checked me in. I phoned the Duffs seeking news of Annabel. Kathleen, Dr. Sam Duff's wife, explained that the doctor was on duty at Hull General Hospital. To my great relief Kathleen had spoken with Annabel after the raid and all was well. The Wrens' quarters were in Willerby, on the outskirts of Hull, a safe distance from the targeted dock area.

I awoke at dawn and after an early breakfast sought out the office of the RNO (Resident Naval Officer) in the nearby Royal Dock Area.

The area is dominated by the famous Grimsby Dock Tower. Three hundred and nine feet high, it was built in 1849 and provided water pressure to the Dock lock gates. It survived World War II bombing as the Luftwaffe used it as a reference point, to fly due west to Liverpool.

The buildings in the Dock area are Victorian in age and architecture. It was in one of these I found the RNO's office.

A happy chance led me to Commander Peter Westbrook, the Resident Naval Officer. He was a friend of Commander Reid, the Training Commander at Portsmouth Barracks. In peacetime they had served on the same ship with visits to Nassau. Like Commander Reid he remembered the dances arranged by the ladies of the I.O.D.E. (Imperial Order of the Daughters of the Empire).

I could not help reflecting on the strange workings of fate: by dancing with visiting Naval Officers and, maybe, exchanging kisses in the moonlight, the kind ladies of the I.O.D.E. in Nassau had smoothed the future pathway of a

Bahamian son. The Commander seemed in no hurry to end his reminiscences of Nassau. When he paused to light a cigarette I asked, "Sir, what is the news of LCT 527?"

He said, "LCT 527 arrived in Immingham several days ago for damage assessment. After her service in the Mediterranean extensive repairs and refitting are necessary. This will take place in the Royal Dock here in Grimsby. On her arrival, and prior to docking, you will officially assume command so that the present crew can be discharged to enjoy some hard-earned rest."

The Commander then spoke of amenities in Grimsby, in particular the Naval Officers Club and the well-stocked Public Library. During my stay in Grimsby I was often the recipient of his guidance and generosity. At his insistence I frequented the RNO premises as LCT 527 was dry docked nearby.

Chapter 2

MEETING WITH ANNABEL

Annabel had phoned in my absence with an invitation to tea at the Wrens' Quarters. I had not seen her for almost a year so it was with some excitement that I took the train from Grimsby to New Holland. There at the end of a 400-metre pier I boarded the P.S. Lincoln Castle for the crossing of the Humber Estuary to Hull's Victoria Pier.

Built in 1920, the Lincoln Castle was the last coal-burning paddle steamer to operate in Britain. The crossing took more than the usual twenty minutes as we ran on to a sand bank exposed by falling tide.

My concern with being late intensified as I took a bus and endured numerous stops along the way. Finally, a kind conductress let me off with a cheerful, "There you are love, the Wrens are just across the street."

A long entranceway led through landscaped gardens to a large three-storied house. There was no one about and I made my way across a lawn toward an oak tree under which were several deck chairs. Suddenly, there was the sound of running feet and Annabel, who had been lying in wait, threw herself into my arms. We kissed in a timeless embrace. She turned, we looked at each other in silence and then embraced again, the moment too wonderful for words.

She led me by the hand toward the chairs under the oak tree. Sunlight filtered through the branches and across her lovely face. We looked at each other and I said, "My darling Annabel, is it really you or am I dreaming?"

She replied, "If there weren't twenty pairs of eyes staring at us I'd kiss you so passionately you'd know that I'm real."

I turned and looked toward the house. There was a flutter of curtains on several windows. Annabel laughed, "My friends knew you were coming and they're checking you out."

We sat and she said, "There is so much to say, but it must wait." Then, with an impish look, she added, "I have a surprise for you, a new friend, someone you know, who admires you."

I shrugged in bewilderment. 'I'll be back in a few minutes," she said, hurrying toward the house.

I sat with my tea watching a couple playing croquet on the far side of the lawn and heard the peaceful clatter of mallet against ball. Lilacs were in bloom and all the fragrances of an English spring in the air. The branches of the oak stirred above my head, sunlight dappled the table set for tea, laughter came from within the house and my body was still stirring from Annabel's recent embrace. I mused on the almost unbearable contrast of this peaceful scene and the confusion of the night before: broken bodies, burning buildings and death raining down from the sky.

I was rescued from such dire thoughts by Annabel returning from the house. She was accompanied by another girl. They were both laughing.

I stood in astonishment. I recognized the girl immediately. She was Maureen Dooley of Londonderry. We embraced while Annabel explained that Maureen, also in Signals, had been posted to Hull just a few weeks before. The two became good friends immediately. I had told Annabel earlier of my friendship with the Dooleys and of the tragic loss of Patrick, Maureen's fiancé.

We sat with our tea and chatted. Maureen had visited Londonderry recently and all was well with her family.

Our conversation was interrupted by a gaggle of Wrens approaching the table. "You're about to be inspected," warned Annabel. I stood and introductions followed, with animated chatter whirling about my head. They were off duty, uniforms discarded for pretty dresses, in a joyous mood and soon, like a flock of restless birds, they fluttered away across the lawn. We watched as they laughed and cavorted, flinging their arms upward, as if about to take flight.

Too soon it was time to leave. I said goodbye to Maureen, with promises that we would meet again. Annabel walked with me to the waterfront and a more convenient bus route to the Ferry Dock.

We spoke excitedly of the Duff's kind offer that we stay in their country cottage for the coming weekend. The Duffs would drive us there on Friday and Kathleen Duff would return for us on Monday morning. Maureen had kindly agreed to take over Annabel's duties for the weekend.

Annabel and I were reluctant to part and sat on a bench holding hands and looking across the sparkling waters of the Humber. Numerous small boats were homeward bound, followed by flocks of shrieking seagulls in their never-ending search for food.

During our year apart we had both discovered the poetry of W.H. Auden. I now quoted an appropriate verse from one of his poems:

> I'll love you dear, I'll love you
> Till China and Africa meet

And the river jumps over the mountain
And the salmon sing in the street.

Annabel responded with:

I'll love you till the ocean
Is folded and hung up to dry
And the Seven Stars go squawking
Like geese about the sky.

Finally, with sunset approaching it was prudent that I get on a bus to the ferry terminal for the last crossing to New Holland and the train to Grimsby.

The next day I was at the Royal Docks at 1600h having been warned of LCT 527's arrival from Immingham. I walked through the dry dock area and, as when joining LCT 801 in Port Glasgow, was astonished at the apparent disorder: great stacks of steel, ladders in various sizes, puddles of water, chain hoists and a maze of hoses and electric leads.

I found LCT 527 huddled against the dockside awaiting entry to the dry dock on the following morning. My first reaction was of dismay. Months of service without a refit and landings in the Mediterranean had taken a heavy toll: the funnel slightly askew, guard rails missing, just one Oerlikon gun and, no doubt, hidden defects to hull and motors.

I was invited aboard and clambered down a steep ladder to be greeted by the Commanding Officer, Lieutenant John Sutcliffe and Sub Lieutenant Noble, the First Lieutenant.

Over drinks Lt. Sutcliffe gave a brief account of their adventures in the Med. While I had been stooging around in LCTs in the Clyde, generally enjoying myself, they had survived operations in Salerno, Sicily and Anzio. Now they were eager to hand over the craft and proceed on their well-deserved leave.

As the craft was already under control of the Dockmaster, Lt. Sutcliffe and I were able to complete the handing over with minimal formalities. While dismayed at her battered appearance, my pride in a first command was intact. When LCT 527 was launched again I would be astride a proven war horse.

Chapter 3

THE WINDY HILL

Breathless we flung us on the windy hill,
Laughed in the sun and kissed the lovely
grass.
You said, "Through glory and ecstasy we
pass
Wind sun and earth remain, the birds sing
still
And when we die, all's over that is ours.
And life burns on through other lovers other
lips."
--------- Then you suddenly cried and turned
away.

Rupert Brooke

We set off with the Duffs in the afternoon. To Annabel's delight the children, Kathy and little Sam, nestled between us on the back seat.

Sam drove the less-traveled roads. There were few people about. Homing cows were glimpsed across the fields making their way to barns and cottages folded into the wooded hills. We passed through Aylesby, Grasby, Somerby and Laceby; the "-by" ending a Scandinavian word for farm, evidence of Viking occupation a thousand years before.

We lingered awhile in Laceby. An arched timeworn stone bridge led across a narrow burbling stream to the village green. Clutching our hands little Sam and Kathy pulled us laughing onto the grass. Doves and pigeons flew from the surrounding woods. It seemed that here in this ancient countryside, behind the crenellated walls of centuries, we could not be harmed.

About thirty miles inland some prehistoric geological aberration had thrust a plateau above the surrounding wold, transformed during the long, slow sweep of time into a woodland sanctuary. Leafy footpaths led upward through ancient trees, home to squirrels and rooks.

The Duff cottage on the upper slope was surprisingly large and well-appointed, an extension of their spacious Grimsby house. The garden on three sides looked out to a mosaic of fields, woods and far-off villages. On the fourth side a meadow sloped upward to the grass-covered summit, looking across a great sweep of curved horizon. At times cold salty winds from the east blew across the intervening countryside, reminder of a cruel sea that lay in wait.

The cottage was stone built; a spacious living area and kitchen on the ground floor and bedrooms and baths on the second floor. While Kathleen and Annabel prepared tea Sam and I brought in wood for the fireplace.

After tea the Duffs returned to Grimsby. Parting had a touching, traumatic moment. Little Sam and Kathy clung tearfully to Annabel but were calmed by hugs and kisses and promises of other visits. They waved goodbye from the back window of the car as Sam drove slowly away.

Darkness seeped slowly from the east bringing with it a cold wind. We sat in front of a blazing fire savouring the wonder of being together. We were in a safe place, the war could not touch us, there was no haste.

But suddenly, we could no longer deny the demands awakened by our sensual caresses. An almost unbearable gathering of sensations brought us to our feet. We looked wild-eyed at each other, a look compounded of tenderness, submission and urgent need. Annabel shouted, "The last one in bed is a monkey."

We scrambled up the stairs, discarding clothing along the way and flung our naked bodies on to the bed. Annabel lay breathless. I knelt astride her. 'You're a darling monkey", she whispered with a smile, reaching up with both arms to gently pull me downward onto her welcoming body.

After a late breakfast we climbed to the summit, an ascent so steep that at times we were on all fours. The western slope, warmed by the midday sun, provided shelter from the cold wind that swept up the eastern slope.

We sat on the grass, our backs against a hummock, and gazed westward across the heartland of England. A flock of gulls, white wings motionless, rode the east wind, to settle on a distant, freshly ploughed field.

Hidden by distance were Sheffield, Leeds and the great sprawl of Manchester; manufacturing centres, vital to England's survival. A hundred miles away on the western coast was Liverpool, the anchor for England's lifeline to North America; defiant, though often targeted by German bombers.

Somewhere in the middle was the Peak District National park, 550 square miles of nature preserve; a moorland of friendly footpaths, gloomy cliffs and rocky hillsides, once a royal hunting ground. High Peak at 636 feet marked the beginning of the Pennine Way, a walking trail, winding its way through England to the far north of Scotland.

"When it's all over let's walk the Pennine Way," said Annabel. "We'll do that," I said, "and we'll voyage to the Galapagos, go around Cape Horn and climb Mount Kilimanjaro—but first we'll go home."

"Home is over there," I said, pointing to the west, "three thousand miles beyond that cloud." Annabel leaned closer, her head on my shoulder. "Sometimes it seems beyond my reach," she said. "When the bombs are exploding and death is nearby I'm terrified and think I'll never see home again."

I drew her nearer to me and kissed her lovely face now wet with tears. I knew that she was not crying for herself alone but for the agony of four years of war, for the fear that dreams might never become reality. There were tears in my own eyes obscuring sky and trees and, I wished for a magical phrase to dispel her sadness, to let her know how much I loved her and to assure her that the war would soon end—but in a little while she was smiling again as we watched a robin, nesting in the trees below, attack a larger intruding magpie.

The hummock against which we lay was in a small grass-covered hollow. Warmth oozed from the earth, the only sound a far-off cuckoo's cry, the valley a moving pattern of shadows, as clouds crossed the sun. We had scarcely slept the night before and now, holding each other closely, drifted downward into a velvet abyss, in which there were no wars.

We returned to the cottage before sunset. Our remaining time together now suddenly seemed immensely precious, to be unraveled slowly; each segment a treasure, stored in memory; to be repossessed when we were apart.

We danced barefooted and hummed the tunes of "Lily of Laguna", "We'll Meet Again" and "Danny Boy." The lines from "The White Cliffs of Dover" were comforting:

There'll be bluebirds over
The white cliffs of Dover
Tomorrow, just you wait and see
There'll be love and laughter
And peace forever after
Tomorrow when the world is free.

We relived funny events from our childhood, named our future children, quoted from our favourite poets and marvelled at the sweet fury and trembling tenderness of our lovemaking; a joyful, physical manifestation of a boundless spiritual love, without which our lives would be desolate. We did not sleep until early dawn.

At breakfast the next morning we spoke of our desire to marry but agreed that circumstances now demanded a postponement. The long planned landing on the coast of France seemed imminent and leave to naval personnel would be curtailed.

On returning to Grimsby I took the train with Annabel to New Holland and thence by ferry to Hull's Victoria Pier. We were mostly silent throughout the journey, our weekend together having wrought a closeness that made parting too distressing for chatter. As the train rattled along the coast, we sat closely together, holding hands and looking across the waters of the Humber. I remembered a line by the German poet, Rainer Maria Rilke:

I hold this to be the highest fulfillment of a
bond between two people: that each protects
the solitude of the other.

We borrowed some time by having coffee and cinnamon buns at the Victoria Pier Café and sat for a while on a terrace looking across the busy Humber, a fortuitous delay, as we then made plans for Annabel to visit Grimsby later in the week. We would dine and then stay at the Royal Hotel,

Annabel returning to Hull the following morning. With this to come we parted in a cheerful mood. Annabel smiled and waved as the bus moved off.

Chapter 4

GRIMSBY DOCKYARD

On returning to Hull I went to Royal Naval Docks. LCT 527, now a steel hulk sitting on girders, was diminished by being on land. I could not muster any pride of command.

The main engines had been hoisted out through cavernous holes in the deck. Both Oerlikon guns were missing. There were dockyard mateys everywhere, either bolting something down or cutting steel plates; the welders' tools chattering away with ominous hissing noises and emitting showers of sparks. Bits and pieces of the craft were scattered nearby as if tossed there by an angry giant: steel ladders, voice pipes, steel doors, handrails, rope and steel cables.

I felt in the way and retreated to my room at the Royal Hotel. I thought I'd take a short kip but did not awaken until late afternoon, my body catching up on sleep lost on the weekend. I wondered how Annabel was faring.

The next morning I met with Bill Partridge, the yard foreman, and Commander Westbrook in the RNO office at the Royal Dock. We went over the works list and discussed some improvements for our greater comfort. These included two cabins for me and the First Lieutenant, and some changes in the crew's quarters.

The two proposed cabins, each to be eight-feet by twelve-feet, would take up a portion of the space designed as a troop shelter. This was a reasonable alteration as when troops were carried they were few in number, seemed to live in their vehicles and were usually on board for short periods.

Later, it turned out, we often ferried cargo or vehicles to the Normandy beaches from ships anchored just offshore, with no need for troop accommodation on board.

Mr. Partridge seemed eager to please and made several useful suggestions. He gave me a sly wink when I told him how useful a wheelbarrow or two would be on the hundred-feet-long tank deck.

At my request we climbed a series of ladders to inspect the area below deck designated as crew's quarters, in which ten to twelve men would sleep and eat. It stretched 38 feet, the entire width of the beam, with two portholes on each side.

Mr. Partridge agreed to provide extra storage shelves and a large corner bin in which hammocks could be stored when not in use, thus providing better daytime use of available space.

He also promised to improve the crew's washing and lavatory facilities by their relocation to the portside, one wall of which would have a porthole. The entrance to this would be a wooden door instead of a canvas curtain.

In the meantime the crew began arriving in Grimsby. With the help of Commander Westbrook, the RNO, they were accommodated in various hostels, to await the launching of our craft.

Peter Walker, the First Lieutenant, arrived in due course – in naval jargon usually referred to as "Number One" or "Jimmy the One." Peter, a Londoner, turned out to be most competent and always available to ease the burden of command. We became close friends and later on, when I recommended him for the Commanding Officer's Course, refused to leave 527.

I arranged that Peter be given an adjoining room at the Royal Hotel. Being nearby we could thus better consult on matters relating to 527's launching. The relative luxury of the Royal Hotel could also be enjoyed for a few days before enduring the confined quarters of a landing craft.

We had frequent meetings with Petty Officer Bates, the Engineer Officer. It always seemed more convenient to meet in the Royal Hotel Bar.

P.O. Bates, from Boston, just 40 miles away, was given my permission, until 527's launching, to go home by bus at day's end. His wife was in great distress, her only brother, a RAF pilot, having been reported missing in a bombing mission over Germany.

Annabel's planned overnight visit was now a poignant memory. We met at the Grimsby train station. She wore a blue dress and a seashell necklace. As always I was filled with wonder at her beauty and proudly escorted her into the hotel's dining salon. Heads turned in her direction, as a discerning headwaiter led us across the room to a secluded corner. We held hands across the candlelit table. I looked into her lovely face and whispered, "I am a very lucky man."

After dinner we went to my room. We avoided mention of the sombre implications of parting on the eve of the dreaded Channel landing which seemed to be imminent, the exact time and destination known only to the High Command.

There was laughter and a few tears as we each sought to reassure the other that our separation would be of short duration. We held each other and talked unhurriedly until long after midnight, reconfirming with words and caresses that our love would survive whatever dangers might lay ahead.

My last visit with her was at tea in the Wren hostelry garden. Her friends, including Maureen Dooley, were there. We endured their presence with politeness, wanting only to be left alone. Walking to the bus stop gave us a brief time together. On the way we made a pact intended to make parting easier. In retrospect, there was no easy way to part.

As agreed, when my bus approached Annabel and I embraced and then turned away. Annabel walked off without looking back. I found a seat and closed my eyes until the bus moved away.

Chapter 5

GETTING READY FOR SEA

L CT 527 was now afloat. After the major overhaul she looked like a new ship. There were many improvements including two new Paxmann diesel engines, two Oerliken anti- aircraft guns and a new bow ramp. A complete paint job covered minor blemishes.

The crew was on board and for two or three days were busy with stores being delivered, checked and placed in appropriate lockers. Ship's routine was established and interaction between the various crew members evolving satisfactorily.

Peter and I were pleased with our new cabins. Each was fitted with double bunks, shelves, hanging space for clothes and a small writing space, with a bookshelf above. We shared a shower and lavatory. There were smiles from the crew when they discovered the improvements on their mess deck.

I sought out Bill Partridge, the yard foreman, to thank him for his many courtesies, and the improvements he had made. As a small token I gave him a bottle of scotch whiskey.[1] He shook my hand and said, "Well Skipper, I

---

[1] Peter and I, both over 21, had wasted no time in purchasing our official monthly allowance of six bottles per officer per month, to be enjoyed socially when in port. The 12 bottles, four each of scotch whiskey, rum and gin, were now stored. In practice we never drank at sea except medicinally. Non-commissioned crew were eligible for a daily tot of

have a gift for you as well. It's a surprise and you'll find it on board." Later I found that he had left two wheelbarrows on board for our use on the tank deck.

I made time for a farewell visit with the Duffs. I wanted to assure them that Annabel and I would never forget their kindness. My visit coincided with Little Sam and Kathy's bedtime. They gave me goodnight hugs with instructions that I pass them on to "Auntie Annabel", who sadly was on duty in Hull.

Finally, on a sunny morning, with an Engineer Officer on board, we headed up river for engine and speed trials. The Engineer Officer, for a time, was on the bridge with me, giving orders through the voice pipe to P.O. Bates in the engine room below. We easily reached the 10-knot maximum speed. I made certain we did not run on shore or demolish another ship.

I gave Peter the opportunity, under my supervision, to con the craft for the first time. His orders through the voice pipes to the helmsmen in the wheelhouse below and to P.O. Bates in the engine room, showed that he had been well-trained, a great comfort to me as we began our voyage.

Engine trials successfully completed, we tied up at Immingham docks for the night. The Engineer Officer took a bus back to Grimsby.

Two more procedures before sailing took place the following day. Firstly, the ship was "degaussed" (usually referred to as "wiping"), a means of demagnetizing the

___

rum at sea. On joining a ship non-commissioned crew were classified as G, T or U.A. G's for Grog were those 21 years or older and given a daily tot (about 1-1/2 oz) of rum, often 140 proof. T's were Temperate for non-drinkers; at one time paid an extra six pence per day. U.A.'s were under age (less than 21), in well-ordered ships given limeade instead, hence the sobriquet "Limey".

craft, it thus being made less vulnerable to magnetic mines and magnetic torpedoes.

Swinging the compass was also necessary after a launching. This required patiently conning the craft in increments of five to ten degrees, through the entire circle of 360 degrees, adjustments to the compass being made throughout the turn. Often it was necessary to repeat the 360 degree turn.

Now, "being in all respects ready for sea" we were given orders to sail south the following morning.

P.O. Bates made a hasty visit to Boston to see his grieving wife. He returned at midnight, quite distressed. It was evident that he needed to confide in someone.

It was a mild starlit night and we sat for awhile on the bridge. Bates was worried about his wife, now grief-stricken by news that her missing RAF brother had been killed with all the plane's crew.

Before returning to Grimsby he had arranged that his mother move in to help his wife and their two young children. I could do little to help beyond listening sympathetically. When he seemed calmer I suggested that we get some sleep before our early morning departure.

My last minute duties ruled out a visit with Annabel. We spoke on the phone. As our parting was inevitable, we were both determined to be composed, not allowing our dreads to surface.

Chapter 6

HEADING SOUTH

Peter and I were on the bridge at 0800 hours. With all hands at their stations and the engines running smoothly I ordered, "Single up to a breast".

The usual sniggers caused by this suggestive command were well hidden. All ropes connecting the ship to the dock were taken aboard, except the breast, a single rope amidship.

The thrust of the current moved the bow slightly away from the dock. I nodded to Peter and he ordered, "Cast Off."

With "Slow ahead port" to the Engine Room and "Starboard fifteen" to the helmsman we moved slowly away. The space between ship and dock widened and we entered the marked channel of the Humber, leading to the open sea.

Soon we were offshore from Grimsby, the Dock Tower its dominant feature. This landmark, visible from twenty miles inland, is also one of the last sights on leaving Grimsby.

We passed Cleethorpes to starboard and, with Spurn Head misty on the port quarter, were now in the open sea. Though a calm day with a few fluffy white clouds against the blue sky, the enormity and power of the North Sea were evident; occasional spray across the bow a reminder of power held in check.

Confined between the coasts of Northwestern Europe and Great Britain, the North Sea often dares to imitate its big brother, the North Atlantic. It seeks to be as cold and as cruel. Moreover, because it is shallower, its surface, when disturbed by frequent storms, can be singularly savage. Its fearsome reputation amongst mariners is well deserved.

I had taken the first watch and was on the bridge, suitably clothed, enjoying the clean cold air on my face. It was time to get on with the main purpose of my training: command of a war craft. Though a 200 feet long motorized barge, LCT 527 had her place in a long tradition that began when mankind first ventured on the sea.

The sea was in my blood and bones, genetic input as recent as my father, Captain Maurice Thompson of the three-mast sailing ship "Alma R", once engaged in trading and rum-running on the Gulf and Atlantic Coasts of North America.

I reflected on mankind's fascination with the sea, celebrated in myth and fable; notably Homer's 8th Century BC epic poem of Odysseus and his voyages. Absent from home for twenty years he wandered around the Aegean Sea, fighting the Trojans, enduring hardships and trying to get home to Penelope his beautiful and faithful wife.

As I looked astern toward the Humber, now below the horizon, where I had left Annabel, the analogy was clear: my Penelope awaited my return as I began this voyage into the unknown.

Our rendezvous with a southbound convoy off the Norfolk Coast was now interrupted by a sudden change of speed.

Eastern Track of LCT527

Petty Officer Bates came on the bridge to report a problem with the starboard engine. He assured me that mechanical help was available in Boston, his hometown now just twenty miles away.

We thought it prudent to proceed on the port motor only. After a six-hour run through shallow waters known as The Wash, we anchored at the entrance to a five-mile long canal which led to Boston. The next morning with an obligatory pilot on board we began a surreal transit through the flat countryside. The bridge of 527 towered above the banks of the narrow canal. We looked down on curious farm workers and equally curious cows, just a hundred feet away.

The crew was delighted as they exchanged greetings with several buxom members of the Woman's Land Army. As we left them astern Stoker Lewis shouted, "We'll see you tonight in Boston." His mates fell about with laughter when one of the girls responded with a mono-digital gesture.

We tied up near the Boston Stump, a tall church tower dominating the small town. Within an hour P.O. Bates arranged mechanical assistance and by early afternoon the problem with the starboard engine had been corrected; too late to exit the canal until the following morning. P.O. Bates requested and was granted overnight shore leave, to be with his wife.

Peter and I climbed many steps to the top of the Boston Stump. The fen land stretched to the western horizon, a pastoral patchwork of fields and canals, unbroken by any elevation.

Looking seaward, the waters of the Wash, five miles away, shimmered in the afternoon sun. This shallow body of water, an indentation in the coastlines of Norfolk and Lincolnshire, is a geologic extension of previous marshland. By drainage and construction of extensive sea banks, many thousands of acres are now suitable for cultivation of crops.

The next morning at 0900 hours, we left Boston. Betty, P.O. Bates wife, came to the dockside to say farewell. She seemed quite composed. I was startled when she embraced me warmly and said, "Thank you, thank you, sir". This somewhat effusive greeting reinforced a lurking suspicion. Did P.O. Bates orchestrate the problem with the starboard engine and its swift repair so that he could overnight in Boston, to further console his grieving wife?

I decided that the situation dictated caution. At some future time I would be enlightened. In the meantime we were again heading south and I was grateful to have a competent engineer, now less distressed by his family tragedy.

Chapter 7

THE FOLLY INN

Boston was now astern. We made our way down the canal toward The Wash. To minimize disturbance of the enclosed waters and damage to the canal banks we went at slow speed. Cultivated fields stretched off on both sides, a peaceful pastoral scene, the flatness relieved by hedgerows and an occasional green coppice. Farm workers on distant fields leaned on their hoes and gazed at our leisurely passing. It seemed that the land was reluctant to give us up to the sea.

Finally, we were in The Wash and having said goodbye to the pilot, increased speed toward the open sea. Rounding the bulge of the Norfolk coast we headed south.

I arranged that all the seamen, with supervision by Number One, have a spell at the wheel. We wanted to ensure that in the vastness of the open sea, without fixed markers, all hands were proficient at steering by compass.

With Great Yarmouth abeam to starboard an embarrassed P.O. Bates came on the bridge to suggest that we put in to Lowestoft just five miles away. He was not satisfied with the performance of the starboard engine.

From the bridge, all seemed well with our progress but I, of course, deferred to my engineer's judgment and we tied up for the night. The next day, after inspections and consultation with local engineers, we were assured that there was no serious problem. We had only to remember that the engines were new and to use caution during the running-in period. I was now somewhat contrite and no longer in doubt that our unscheduled visit to Boston had been mechanically warranted.

We left at dawn the following morning for the ninety-mile run to Southend. The weather worsened and we rammed our way through surging waves, some of the crew pale-faced with seasickness, retching on to the wet deck. It was with relief that in the cold and windy darkness of evening, we finally came alongside in Southend.

The next day we joined up with a convoy for the onward passage through the Straits of Dover. Nightfall came early in the blustery weather and we endured an interminable nightmare as we struggled to keep in sight the dim blue stern light of the craft ahead.

Dawn was welcomed and, with the weather moderating, we continued west along the south coast, passing Dungeness, Beachy Head and Selsey Bill to starboard. As we approached the Isle of Wight we were amazed at the enormous amount of ship traffic. We were soon to be enlightened.

With ships at anchor and other ships of all sizes approaching from various directions it was daunting to enter the congested waters of Cowes Roads. We waited interminably for permission to enter the harbour of Cowes, the mouth of the Medina River. Coming alongside a pier at East Cowes, we discovered, with a mixture of chagrin and relief that the Big Landing had begun on the beaches of Normandy.

We had missed the cutting edge of events, unaware that in the weeks to follow we would more than compensate by numerous crossings to Normandy and weeks of ferrying cargoes to the beaches from ships anchored offshore.

For some unknown reason we were now instructed to proceed up the Medina River. We anchored off the Folly Inn and were welcomed by the proprietor and habitués. A bibulous evening followed, in cautious celebration of the landings in progress. We could not forget the slaughter on the beaches of Dieppe and Anzio.

It took just a couple of pints to develop a fondness for the Inn's special brand of ale. Suddenly Peter and I and the ship's crew had many friends.

The next morning, to Peter's delight, we were invited to tie up at the Inn's waterfront. 527, almost two hundred feet in length, dwarfed the narrow frontage. Sally, the inn-keeper's lovely daughter may well have arranged this move. It was obvious that she and Peter had taken a fancy to each other.

In every corner of England there was rejoicing that finally, four years after being pushed into the sea at Dunkirk, we had now returned to France. This joy was evident at the Folly Inn. Pub hours were ignored. Crowds of Folly Inn patrons overflowed onto LCT 527; with drinks in hand they leaned on the railings or formed groups wherever there was deck space.

Sally's father and I took a bottle of Scotch whiskey to the bridge. From this vantage point, we saw Sally and Peter, hand-in-hand, make their way along a woodland path, that led to the hills above. "A good lad, I trust?" he asked, looking me in the eye. "One of the best," I said, "one of the very best."

Someone brought a gramophone and there was dancing on the tank deck. Soon an impromptu sing-a-long was in full swing, with current favourite tunes: "There is a Tavern in the Town," "Cruising Down the River" and "Roll out the Barrel." Everyone joined in when "The White Cliffs of

Dover" was played. This quiet inlet of the Medina River pulsated with happy sounds.

As more drink was consumed the singing became raucous. Their Lordships at the Admiralty would have shuddered at my laxity as Commander of HMS 527.[1]   When a spill occurred in a wheelbarrow race on the tank deck I decided that restraint was needed. I ordered the engines started, as if about to depart. Everyone trooped off to continue the celebration onshore.

Two days later this interlude was interrupted by orders to proceed to Portsmouth for loading. I was secretly relieved as, increasingly, I felt left out of this momentous undertaking for which we had trained so arduously.

There were fond farewells as we cast off, Peter looking shoreward until Sally and other well wishers merged with the shoreline.

---

[1]Perhaps not, considering the special circumstances. I believe that my former boss, Lord Mountbatten of Combined Operations Command would have taken part. I met him at Government House in Nassau after the War and he was amused when I told him of our celebrations at the Folly Inn.

Chapter 8

FIRST CROSSING

A short run down the Medina River brought us to Cowes and into the Solent. This waterway, between the Isle of Wight and Portsmouth, was teeming with ships, naval and merchant marine. Those not at anchor were going in various directions, all part of a multifarious support system for the Allied troops in Normandy.

Mooring to a trot buoy,[1] we were eventually directed to a loading hard, a sloping concrete ramp, onto which we lowered our heavy bow door. We watched with alarm as the drivers of monster Churchill tanks manoeuvred them through the door and along the tank deck into two-abreast positions. All tanks were then securely screwed down to prevent movement while at sea. Then with the door winched up and secured we were ready for sea.

We left Portsmouth and joined a flotilla of LCTs to the east of the Isle of Wight. The tanks aboard were of British Thirtieth Corp., some of their crew already looking pale around the gills as 527 thrust through the moderate swell.

A LCT Mark 4 unloading lorries on a beach demonstrates the scale and size of the landing craft. It was capable of carrying 12 loaded 3-ton trucks or 6 of the heaviest Churchill tanks, fitting two abreast in its cargo area. The Mark 4 was 187' long with a beam of 39'.

---

[1]A buoy capable of accommodating more than one ship.

Our flotilla was then directed to an Assembly Area southeast of the Isle of Wight. As we approached, the sea around to the horizon was dotted with ships of all sizes, a fraction of the 6,483 strong assembly on D-Day.

On D-Day there were nine battleships, 23 cruisers, 104 destroyers, 71 corvettes, 2,285 converted liners and merchantmen, and thousands of landing craft and ships – from LCVPs carrying one or two vehicles and personnel, up to 300-feet long LSTs, ships of several thousand ton capacity.

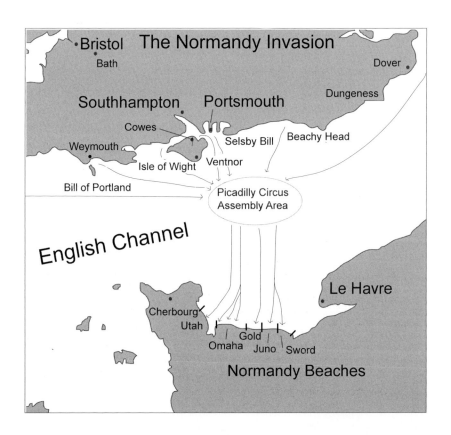

The initial assault consisted of 176,475 men, 20,000 vehicles, 1,500 tanks and 5,000 planes. For many weeks thereafter hundreds of thousands of troops and an inexhaustible supply of vehicles and material flooded across the Channel. There was minimum defence from German fighter planes, now reduced to 109, ineffectual against the Allied 5,000 planes.

Tony Davies, the Army Captain in charge of the tanks and their crews, visited me on the bridge. They had been training for many months and were now ready to join their fellow soldiers on the Normandy coast. After awhile Tony admitted to feeling "jolly queasy". "Must be something I ate," he explained, as he excused himself. I suggested that he lie down in my cabin with the door left open.

A line of LCT Mark 4's crossing the channel to the beaches of Normandy in France. The landing craft assembled in an area designated as "Picadilly Circus" to the southeast of the Isle of Wight before making the crossing..

Directed by the Command Centre of the Asssembly Area our Flotilla and other ships proceeded South through a swept channel toward the beaches of Normandy, between Cape Barfleur and the Seine Estuary.

When about twenty miles off the beaches some of the leading craft veered off to port toward the other British beaches: Juno and Sword. Our flotilla continued on to Gold Beach, which covered about five miles of shoreline; Arromanches, a short distance away, being the principal village.

Max Hastings in *Overlord*, a masterly book on D-Day, writes:

> At the initial landing on D-Day there were serious difficulties on Gold Beach. At this most westerly of the British beaches the British forces were met by furious fire from German bunkers, little scarred by previous bombardment. A survivor remembered "noise noise noise," a continuous roar of gunfire, much of it from Allied bombardment ships.
>
> Some of the landing craft on approaching the beaches struck mines. Survivors swam for the shore and crouched in shallow water as enemy bullets rippled the sand.
>
> Historians might say that the Gold landing was easier than expected and that casualties were light but for those present there were periods of violent intensity and horror. It would not have helped them to know that the American experience on Omaha was more terrible in scale.
>
> Much was accomplished by those who survived — and by those who lost their

lives. "By 10:30 am the British sector had landed fifteen Infantry battalions, seven Commandoes, seven Tank regiments, two Engineer Assault regiments and scores of supporting units. Almost everywhere along the British line the German coast positions had been rolled up.

On approaching the beach we passed battleships at anchor, occasionally pumping out 15-inch shells onto designated targets inland. Though some distance from the ships the thunderous roar of their guns and the belching of smoke and flames was awesome.

The Mulberry Harbour was by-passed and we headed for the King sector of the Gold area.

A British LCT Mark 4 proceeding to one of the beaches at Normandy under cover of the U. S. Battleship Arkansas.

Stephen Ambrose, historian of note, describes the Mulberry Harbours:

The idea of towing prefabricated ports across the Channel was astonishing. By the end of 1943 thousands of British workers were helping to construct the artificial ports (code name Mulberries) and the breakwaters to shelter them. The "docks" consisted of floating piers connected by treadway to the beach. The piers were devised so that the platform, or roadway, could slide up and down with the tide on four posts that rested on the sea bottom. The breakwater (code name Phoenix) combined hollow, floating concrete caissons about six stores high with old merchant ships. Lined up end to end off the French coast, the ships and Phoenixes were sunk by opening their sea cocks. The result: an instant breakwater protecting instant port facilities, in place and ready to go on D-Day plus one.

The Mulberries were not in operation long; a great storm two weeks after D-Day knocked out the American Mulberry and badly damaged the British one. But the great LCT fleet more than made up the difference, raising the question: Was the expenditure of so much material and manpower on building the Mulberries wise?

Russell Weigley's answer is yes. In his book *Eisenhower's Lieutenants: The Campaigns of France and Germany*, he opines:

> Without the prospect of the Mulberries to permit the beaches to function as ports, Churchill and his government would probably have backed away from Overlord after all.

In due course, following semaphore instructions from the Beachmaster, we beached. Two crew members aft

Mulberry Harbour before damage by the storm.

efficiently dropped the kedge anchor. Number One in the bow supervised a timely lowering of the tank doors.

There was great activity on the beach, the wreckage of several vehicles evidence of enemy resistance on D-Day. To our great relief there were no enemy aircraft. In the days following the landings a German Army joke had it that if a plane in the sky was silver it was American, if it was blue it was British, if it was invisible it was German.

Captain Davies on the bridge and Number One in the bow now supervised unloading, the tanks rumbling off to an almost dry landing through just a foot of water. Considering the rising tide I felt happy with our performance.

Captain Davies, still a little pale from his seasickness shook our hands in farewell. "I enjoyed your company," he said, "but your ship was *jolly miserable*". I thought one oxymoron deserved another and called after him, "She's pretty ugly as well."

There were sounds of gunfire inland and the occasional whine of a passing shell from the battleships offshore. The tanks now clattered off across the dunes, some of their crew standing in the turrets and waving goodbye to my crew.

We then executed the naval manoeuvre, at which we all excelled: "Getting to hell away from the beach." With engines in reverse and the capstan winding in the kedge anchor we moved rapidly off the beach and anchored well offshore for the night. In the early morning we joined a flotilla of LCTs for the return voyage to Portsmouth.

On arriving in Portsmouth we tied up to a pier near a loading hard. As orders to load the next morning were expected we turned in early.

Our rest was soon disturbed by the chattering roar of a jet-driven V-1 rocket, the first of Germany's two new instruments of terror – the V-2s would come later.[2]

---

[2]From June 13 to the end of 1944, flying bombs and rockets killed 7,533 and wounded almost 20,000 London civilians. In 1945, 1,705 more were killed and 3,836 wounded. Outside of London, along the route taken by the bombs, 1,097 were killed and 2,765 were wounded during 1944-45.

Having been spared enemy attacks on the Normandy beach we felt affronted that this could happen to us in an English harbour.

The raucous noise increased. There was no time for indignation. The rocket was headed our way with its lethal one ton load of explosive. The crew were still scrambling up from below when suddenly there was an ominous silence. The V-1's motor had stopped. The bomb was heading earthward. Some of us hit the deck, others sat or stood frozen as the bomb plunged into the darkened surface of the harbour.

The water erupted, black smoke roiled upward and a thunderous boom and shock wave kept us crouched on the deck. Fortunately there were no ships at the point of impact or near enough to be damaged.

In about half an hour another rocket was heard, on the same path as the first. It passed directly over 527. When its motor stopped the resulting explosion was muffled by distance.

Sometime after midnight we turned in and slept undisturbed until 0600h.

The next morning we were ordered to a nearby loading yard. There was a repetition of the whole process: loading of vehicles, crossing the Channel to Normandy and unloading on to a beach.

This tedious routine was relieved at times by being detached from a Flotilla, to remain at the beaches, for days or weeks, ferrying vehicles or cargo from anchored ships to the beaches. Or taking on vehicles from a beach and transporting them several miles along the Normandy coast to another beach.

Day and night, often in miserable weather, from June until November LCTs ferried arms and materiel from a seemingly inexhaustible supply in England to the Allied forces, whose needs increased daily, as they fought their way across France and into Germany.

By the end of August the Allies had landed in Normandy 39 divisions of 2,052,299 men, along with 438,471 vehicles and 3,098,259 tons of stores. The Battle of Normandy was over and Allied spearheads were advancing virtually unopposed toward Germany. The human cost was grievous, 209,672 casualties including 36,976 dead; 4,101 allied aircraft and 16,714 aircrew had been lost. (Stephen Badsey: November 1944).

The frequent channel crossings spawned an unofficial "Blue Ribbon" competition, LCT crews vying for the first place in the number of round trips to the beaches. My twenty trips was a modest number. I did however take comfort that, additionally, I spent long periods on detached service along the Normandy coast.

Most LCT Commanders welcomed freedom from the apron strings of a Flotilla. The clearing of enemy minefields, scarcity of enemy ships or planes and our mounting experience encouraged self reliance. Passing weeks brought increasing autonomy and we often crossed the Channel independently, or in company with two or three other craft.

With more than one craft the most senior commander (in terms of date of being commissioned) became the leader.

There were bound to be SNAFUs.[3] A story, perhaps apocryphal or dreamed up by our arch rivals, the pukka Royal Navy Officers, went the rounds: A RNVR[4] LCT skipper crossing independently from Gold Beach to Portland decided that he was lost. By Aldis lamp he signaled another LCT in the distance. "What is my position please?" The response came quickly, "Sorry, I can't help you. I'm RNVR too."

As the weeks unfolded there were voyages of special interest for LCT 527 and her crew — and, lying in wait a cruel fate was poised to strike a mortal blow.

With unreliable telephone service and my frequent cross Channel voyages, I did not speak with Annabel until mid-July. She was in a buoyant mood, echoing the guarded national jubilation.

Enemy bombing raids on the Humber area had ceased and Allied troops, though hard pressed at times, were firmly entrenched in Normandy. Annabel was relieved that my voyages to Normandy were without enemy interference.

We exchanged twenty-third birthday wishes, mine for July 1st, belated, and Annabel's for August 1st, in advance. She planned a weekend at home with her parents, at an early date. Arrangements for our wedding would be made, subject to our being on leave at the same time.

---

[3] SITUATION NORMAL ALL F----D UP

4 Royal Naval Volunteers Reserve

Mail delivery too was unpredictable. On returning from Normandy my first errand ashore was always to check for mail. Shortly after speaking to Annabel in mid-July I received a letter she had written in mid-June.

> My dearest Chester,
>
> I know that you will have mixed feelings about your delayed crossing to Normandy. For me it was the removal of a great burden of dread. I think that you have already tempted fate enough. Be content that you survived greater dangers.
>
> Our troops now seem well-established in France and Jerry bombers no longer target this area. We are hopeful that an end is not far off. There is a feeling of marking time but, of course, the daily routines continue.
>
> Maureen and I have become close friends and I believe this is helpful in her continuing struggle with the loss of Patrick in the North Atlantic. That you survived the Battle of the Atlantic was miraculous and now you are in less danger. We need only endure this final separation before being together for the rest of our lives.
>
> The Anthology you left with me is a great comfort. I feel very close to you when I read our favourite poems. These are often about the sea.

John Masefield in *Sea Fever* writes of an alluring sea:

> I must go down to the seas again, for
> the call of the running tide
> Is a wild call and a clear call that may
> not be denied.
> It's a warm wind, the west wind, full
> of bird's cries,
> I never hear the west wind but tears
> are in my eyes."

I know that you admire Tennyson, especially his "Ulysses." After a glass of wine you are likely to launch into "Come my friends 'tis not too late to seek a newer world," etc., but my Tennyson favourite is the lullaby "Sweet & Low," also about the west wind. I sometimes pretend I'm crooning it to our child.

> Sweet and low, sweet and low,
> Wind of the western sea.
> Low, low, breathe and blow
> Wind of the western sea!
> Over the rolling waters go,
> Come from the dying moon, and
> blow,
> Blow him again to me;
> While my little one, while my pretty
> one, sleeps.'

I'm so happy that you introduced me to Rachel Field's "If once you've slept on an island." It gives me joy to imagine you reading it again.

> If once you have slept on an island
> You'll never be quite the same;

You may look as you looked the day
before
And go by the same old name,
You may bustle about in street and
shop;
You may sit at home and sew,
But you'll see blue water and wheeling
gulls
Wherever your feet may go.
You may chat with the neighbours of
this and that
And close to your fire keep,
But you'll hear ship whistle and
lighthouse bell
And tides beat through your sleep.
Oh, you won't know why, and you
can't say how
Such change upon you came,
But—once you have slept on an
island
You'll never be quite the same!

Perhaps it's time I went to bed holding on
to thoughts of you and me beside a peaceful
Bahamian sea. I'm on duty early tomorrow
morning and will say Good Night now.

We must be apart for a while longer but the
space between us will never be too wide for
me not to touch you. You know that if you
cry out to me I shall always hear you. My
love will enfold you and support you.

Yours always,
Annabel

Chapter 9

THE EGG RUN

"An army marches on its stomach".
Napoleon Bonaparte

By the end of June the Battle for Normandy had taken on a pattern that was to continue for the next three months. The front had widened to about one hundred miles and, by August, involved more that two million men. Use of Le Havre and Cherbourg, ports at the eastern and western ends of the beaches, was still denied to the Allies by a defiant enemy. However, men, armour, ammunition and food, indispensable to waging the war, flowed from England to the Normandy beaches by troop ships, freighters and landing craft.

LCT 527 was now based at the Isle of Portland, on England's south coast. Being island-born I was intrigued and over several afternoons, in company with Peter or P.O. Bates, walked where possible. Some areas, occupied by Navy or Army were off limits. For a small island—four and a half miles long and one and three quarter miles wide—it had some outstanding features. There were three fortified castles. Portland Castle, with walls fourteen feet thick, built by Henry VIII as a defense against French invasion was the most impressive. There were echoes of another time, another kind of war, as we stumbled through its passages.

Coming from The Bahamas, with gentle beaches barely above sea level, I found Portland's coastline most interesting.

Sheer cliffs drop down to an untamed sea where, even on calm and sunny days, huge waves crash and thunder on to the rocky shore below. Some of the most treacherous currents meet at the Bill of Portland, the southern tip of the Isle, making it one of the most hazardous shipping areas of England.

By contrast, the artificial harbour on the Isle's north coast is well-protected. Its six-thousand-feet breakwater is built of the hard white limestone quarried on the Isle. Constructed by convicts in the mid-nineteenth century it is said to be the largest artificial harbour in Britain.

It was at a loading ramp on the south shore of Portland Harbour, on a blustery July afternoon, that we loaded several vehicles of a Canadian Army Quartermaster Corp. The officer in charge, Lieutenant John Delworth, with a fellow officer and several drivers soon made themselves at home on 527. We tied up to a buoy, for an early departure the next morning. During the night a fierce storm blew in and for the next forty-eight hours the Canadians wished they had never seen a landing craft. The night seemed endless, with shouts in the darkness from craft parted from their moorings. To survive they headed into the wind, meanwhile trying to avoid other craft in the crowded harbour.

With dawn the wind force decreased and our Canadian guests hesitantly emerged from their shelters. Some craft without moorings found safety by tying up to a protected dock on the south shore of the harbour; others went to loading ramps, an ebb tide leaving them high and dry and safe. One craft, fortunately without cargo, was swept on to the Weymouth shore.

By day's end the weather had improved, so that we caught up on lost sleep. On the third morning we discovered that the vehicles on board, with various food items for the troops in Normandy included one vehicle designed to preserve eggs. It contained hundreds of boxes of eggs, each box holding 30 dozen eggs.

Normal food rations on LCTs were basic and included powdered eggs, an unappetizing egg substitute also found on Civilian Ration cards. Unless one lived on a farm, eggs were not available.

A kind Fate had thrust upon us a situation that demanded some rearrangement. Some adjustment took place, naturally. Having survived the storm together the Canadians were now our chums, and for the duration of their stay there were eggs in abundance at every meal time: boiled, fried or scrambled.

On the eighteen-hour voyage to Normandy the weather was fine. Lieutenant Delworth was with me on the bridge for several hours. We had much in common, both intending enrollment at a Canadian university when the war was over. My crew and the Canadian soldiers were now great friends, frequent roars of laughter erupting as they exchanged repartee.

We finally beached near Arromanche on Gold Beach. Lieutenant Delworth and I watched from the bridge as his vehicles were maneuvered on to the beach. On leaving, he shook my hand and said, "Thank you for a memorable voyage. I left a small gift in your cabin." I was curious but occupied for awhile with leaving the beach and going alongside a tanker for refueling.

As we set out for Portland I was relieved on the bridge by Peter. He was laughing, "You'll never believe what has happened," he said. I shrugged, "OK Number One, enlighten me." "Lieutenant Delworth left a box of eggs on your bunk and his Sergeant gave P.O. Bates another box."

That was not the end of it. Halfway into the return voyage I discovered that Stoker Halstead had traded a duffel coat for a box of eggs and the truck driver had given my men another box. With only 12 men to feed we now had 120 dozen eggs. On arrival in Portland we became very popular, supplying eggs to other landing craft and nearby ships. At day's end the liberty men went ashore burdened with eggs to hand out to people on the street. As we were in port for only three days I resorted to sending "egg parties" into town to leave eggs on doorsteps.

When retained at the beaches to unload ships anchored offshore, we found their crews were invariably friendly. When, at times, we remained overnight, nestled alongside a freighter, they would include us in their catering. Meals, sumptuous by LCT standards, would be offered—and accepted.

Our contacts with Canadian Army personnel often exposed us to Compo Packs: - Composite Ration Packs[1]—boxes of

---

[1] COMPOSITE RATION PACK   TYPE E
(14 men for one day)   Contents and Suggested Use

BREAKFAST Tea   *3 tins(2 tall, 1 flat, Tea, Sugar & Milk
Powder)
+ Sausage (1 hr)   2 tins
Biscuit   *1 tin
Margarine*   *1 tin
(*items marked thus are also to provide for other meals)
DINNER   +Haricot Oxtail (½ hr)   12 tins
                +Vegetables (3/4 hrs)   2 tins
                +Pudding (1 hr)   3 tins (2 large, 1 small)

tinned rations designed for groups of fourteen men for one day. A daily menu with each box provided breakfast, dinner, tea and supper. For variety there were various types of Compo Packs, designated A to E, everything already cooked, needing only to be heated. Some packs contained surprises: hard candies, chocolate and, if lucky, tinned peaches.

The Americans were equally generous with their sealed boxes of "K" rations, numbered one to ten, each providing a complete change of diet. The records show that during the four weeks following D-Day 60 million boxes of K-rations were shipped to Normandy. Some troops in rear areas had access to ice-cream making machines.

TEA	Tea	- (*see above)
	Biscuit	- (*see above)
	Margarine	- (*see above)
	Sardines	8 tins
SUPPER	Cheese	1 tin
	Biscuit	- (*see above)
EXTRAS	Cigarettes	2 tins (1 round, 1 flat - 7 cigarettes per man)
	Sweets	2 tins (1 tall, 1 flat)
	Salt	- (packed in flat)
	Matches	- (sweet tin)
	Chocolate	1 tin (1 slab per man)
	Soap	1 tablet

DIRECTIONS

Tea, Sugar and Milk Powder – Use a dry spoon and sprinkle powder on heated water and bring to a boil, stirring well. 3 heaped teaspoonfuls to 1 pint of water.

+May be eaten hot or cold. To heat, place unopened tins in boiling water for the minimum period as indicated. Sausage and pudding cut into ½ inch slices, may be fried (using margarine) if preferred.

Chapter 10

A LETTER FROM A FRIEND

It was many and many a year ago,
In a kingdom by the sea,
That a maiden there lived whom you may
know
By the name of Annabel Lee; -
And this maiden she lived with no other
thought
Than to love and be loved by me.

I was a child and she was a child,
In this kingdom by the sea,
But we loved with a love that was more than
love –
I and my Annabel Lee –
With a love that the winged seraphs in
Heaven
Coveted her and me.

Edgar Allen Poe

The 300-mile return trips from Portland to Normandy were relieved by the ship-to-shore shuttles at the beaches. While allowing more independence it involved an endless pattern of taking cargo from ships anchored offshore, beaching, unloading – and then more of the same. Long days would merge into weeks.

On a day in late August we set off for Portland. Hopefully there would be a letter from Annabel awaiting my arrival. With luck we might speak on the phone. On arrival Peter collected the ship's mail. My only letter was from Maureen Dooley. I read it without understanding, and then read it again.

Dear Chester,

It is very difficult to write this letter but someone has to tell you. There is no easy way. I tried several times to reach you by phone. You are probably stuck over in Normandy and Annabel's parents may be too stricken or otherwise unable to communicate.

Annabel was on a bus that was destroyed by a V-1 bomb; all the passengers were killed, nearby houses destroyed with many casualties. It was such bad luck, she was on a long weekend pass and going across London to Waterloo for the train to Guildford. We didn't know about it for two days and all here are terribly sad.

She was so good to me and helped me with my grief. Also, I have not forgotten your help at the time of Patrick's death. You both helped me find the strength to carry on. I now grieve with you and pray that you will find the strength to endure in a world without your Annabel.

With love,
Your friend
Maureen

At first a numbness, a difficulty in breathing, too stricken to rage at the unimaginable odds — that would come later. After four years of war, with an end in sight, a madman's final desperate stroke destroys a random bus crossing a vast city.

Please let it have been a sudden oblivion, Annabel unaware of silent down-rushing death.

A cruel twisted Fate showed its most evil face and robbed Annabel of her rendezvous with Life; with me and our children, beside a warm sea.

Instead, a rendezvous with insatiable Death, already engorged with million upon million of dead English, American, Russian, French, Polish in two World Wars.

Peter found me staring at Maureen's letter and insisted that we walk. I realized later that he intended tiring me to the point of exhaustion. We walked through the streets of Castleton, then upward to the top of 490 feet high Verne Hill, along the precipitous coastline to the Bill of Portland, with its storm-worn caves and seagulls swooping and calling around Pulpit Rock

Peter, sensing my need for solitude, sat some distance away. I gazed at the sea below, retreating across a turbulent surface to the horizon – and beyond to France where armies clashed and men died.

I was sick with self-recrimination. Had I failed her by not writing more often, or arranging, somehow, that we marry? The line from Khalil Gibran was of little comfort: "Ever has it been that love knows not its own depth until the moment of separation."

An aroma of salt-saturated heather and warm earth mingled with spray flung upward by the waves below. I found that I was crying, silently, tears on my checks. Annabel was nearby and I knew that the message in her last letter would sustain me in the days ahead.

> The space between us will never be too wide
> for me not to touch you. You know that if you
> cry out to me I shall always hear you. My love
> will enfold you and support you.

On our return Peter and I paused briefly on the Common, overlooking a Naval Cemetery and the harbour below. Several Wrens in uniform approach across the grass; not a blonde head amongst them but I am momentarily stricken, until, as they pass by, I notice their earthbound gait, unlike Annabel with her distinctive stride, feet seemingly not touching the ground.

I dreaded phoning Annabel's parents but when I finally spoke to Anne I was astonished at her composure. Later, I realized that she was controlling her own grief to better console me. They had tried to reach me and were aware that I was on duty in Normandy. Bill was in touch with the London authorities. A mass burial service, customary in the circumstances, would take place in London. All concerned would be given an opportunity to attend.

Chapter11

A BROKEN BACK

We were ordered onto a loading ramp early the following morning and left harbour by 0900. As we were sailing alone I decided to proceed east along the coast to St. Albans Head before altering course southeast toward the Normandy beaches.

I welcomed being able to keep mind and body active, to work, to somehow dull the sharp edges of misery. The weather conspired to match my mood. An hour into the voyage we ran into heavy winds out of the southeast. I decided against scudding back to Portland.

With St. Albans Head off to port the weather worsened, low menacing clouds with wind blown rain and limited visibility. Peter did a check on the vehicles, to make certain they were securely strapped to the deck. The drivers were sheltering in the tank-deck quarters.

Now bucking a heavy sea, with spray sweeping across the bridge, I decided to head for the Needles, the westerly end of the Isle of Wight, about twenty miles away.

Being deeply laden I thought it prudent to run at half-speed. The change of speed and course eased somewhat the constant ramming through the waves.

Peter joined me on the bridge and for the next five hours 527 wallowed along. Light was fading as we felt our way into shelter on the lee side of The Needles and finally into protected Totland Bay.

Anchoring in about eight fathoms.[1] I thought it prudent to keep the motors running until certain there was no drag on the anchor.

The Canadian Army personnel emerged from their shelters, relieved to be in calm waters but uneasy about another hundred miles to go.

I had not slept the night before and now collapsed onto my bunk. Peter organised anchor watches and prepared for an early morning departure, weather permitting.

During the night the wind shifted to the sou'west and by morning had decreased to a gentle breeze. The Canadians were smiling again. An early start had us rounding The Needles by 0600 and anchored off Gold Beach before nightfall.

A diary kept for the next three days relates the now familiar routines at the beaches.

> Day One. Have hardly had time to breathe since our arrival. As soon as one load is on the beach, back we go to a transport for another load – turn in at midnight, if lucky.
>
> At present we're alongside a transport ship, MT90, taking on vehicles. Soldiers line the ship's side looking toward France, watching their vehicles being loaded, no doubt

---

[1] Although a fathom is now a nautical measure of six feet it was once defined by an Act of Parliament as "the length of a man's arms around the object of his affections". The word derives from the Old English "faethem" which means the embracing arms.

wondering what Fate has in store for them. The shore is indistinct, as the sky is quite overcast today.

Day Two. We're alongside MT92. Have been here over three hours, just three vehicles taken aboard. We're told this is due to a shortage of prisoners of war who help with unloading. A convoy of LCTs came in this morning. Perhaps we'll be sent back with them for more cross-Channel runs.

Day Three. Sent to Juno Beach with a cargo of vehicles, beached at 0915 on an ebbing tide. The Beachmaster was tardy with our unloading and we dried out. At low tide with 527 sitting high and dry I did a casual inspection of the hull. I was alarmed to find on both outboard sides the opening of a vertical seam.

The Beachmaster came to have a look. At the top, the seam opening was about four inches wide, tapering to about half an inch at the craft's bottom. It was clear that 527 had a "broken back".

No one was surprised. LCT 527, one of the earlier Mark 4s, had seen arduous service in the Mediterranean and, most recently, many Channel crossings, in all weathers. No doubt in the Med and certainly in the Normandy crossings we ignored the fact that the craft were not designed to sail in more than Force 4 winds.

There was no evidence of flooding. The steel plates of each waterproof compartment were independent of the steel hull. However, it was evident that the integrity of the hull and consequently the seaworthiness of the craft were jeopardized.

Generally LCTs Mark 4 had shown great resilience due no doubt to their honey-combed construction of many waterproofed sections. There was a case on record of a LCT Mark 4 breaking in half in mid-Channel. The stern half towed the bow back to Portsmouth.

Two days later we were at the far end of Portsmouth Harbour lying with our bow about twelve feet from a mudbank, submerged at high water, its location marked by stakes. In the distance Portsdown Hills, a long stretch of high ground, separated the interior from the coastal strip.

At low tide we gazed across the mud flats, on which flocks of noisy gulls scavenge. Nearby, several other damaged LCTs awaited repairs. Some appeared to be unmanned.

The first day passed without the promised visit by a dock-yard representative. There was a distinct feeling of "out-of-sight, out-of-mind".

On the third day an apologetic civilian appeared. Together, we prepared a defect list. After a couple of whiskies the list was amended to include some items for our greater comfort.

Aboard his launch and about to depart, Cecil—we were now on a first name basis—somewhat hesitantly informed me that, due to overworked repair facilities, we could be waiting around for several days, or even weeks.

Chapter 12

FAREWELL

A phone call to Annie and Bill was timely. They had been trying to get in touch with me. A service for relatives of victims of the V-1 explosion had been arranged, in a small park near the bomb site.

They met me at Waterloo Station, having arrived in London the day before. We rode a taxi through streets lined with other bomb sites; stony rubble marking collapsed buildings, some with intact three-storey sections of wall, still supporting portions of rooms, with surviving staircases reaching skyward or downward to missing floors. In other ruined buildings, tattered wallpaper, shattered windows and mangled furnishings were grim reminders of destroyed households.

Some buildings, with cracked walls, appeared to still offer shelter to those who would otherwise be homeless.

The small neighbourhood park chosen for the service was crowded, the overflow standing in landscaped areas or on the adjoining street; a collection of many huddled family groups, each hoping to receive from the collective grief a softening of individual grief.

My sorrow was more easily borne as Bill and I were both intent on helping Annie. Later, I realised that Annie was determined to be strong for Bill and me. I gained strength from their fortitude and would never forget that the best way to cope with one's own grief is to help a grieving friend.

When the service ended Bill and Annie hurried off to catch a train to Albury. To my surprise, I was joined by Maureen Dooley, who had arrived from Hull, too late to attend the service.

At her suggestion we walked to St. James Park. Leaning against the railing of a bridge across a small lake we watched the stately progression of several swans. I pointed out two or three Bahama ducks, looking quite at home in a flock of larger ducks.

We spoke of inconsequential matters — news from Londonderry, the status of repairs to my craft — each knowing that the other was struggling with irreparable loss: Maureen's Patrick in the vast graveyard of the North Atlantic, my darling Annabel without whom I was diminished. Then, in unison, silently, we turned and held each other; the emotional power of our sorrow temporarily lessened by our embrace.

The sunny afternoon had attracted other walkers. Mothers with prams, paused and chatted, children ran about, playing games and shouting. In secluded leafy areas couples lay entwined, oblivious of curious passers-by.

A small band played cheerful tunes, reflecting upbeat news from our armies in Europe. I rented two deck chairs for threepence each and we sat some distance from the crowd, our backs against a hedge.

Being aware of my fondness for country walks, Maureen now suggested that, when our leaves coincided, we walk, with a group, along Hadrian's wall or the Pennine Way. We would backpack and sleep wherever the day ended, hopefully in farmers' rental cottages or in bed and breakfast accommodation.

Soon, Maureen left, to rendezvous with other Wrens for the return journey to Hull. I made my way to St. Martins-in-the-Fields Church, near Trafalgar Square. I remembered it from two years before as a place of solace; on this sad day a welcome retreat from the London crowds.

A trio of musicians had attracted a small gathering. I sat in a back pew. The violinist of the group chose to play a Mozart sonata. Though musically untutored I was completely captivated. Passages were played with such authority that the notes seemed to be sung instead of bowed.

When the musicians left I stayed on in the empty church and mused on the bleak unfolding of the days and weeks ahead. I realised that, to survive, my movements and behaviour must be dictated by my responsibilities and sense of duty; my feelings of loss kept below the surface.

I took comfort in the certain knowledge that this was what Annabel would want from me.

Chapter 13

AROUND LAND'S END

The day after returning to 527 we were visited by Cecil, our friend from the dockyard. As his launch came alongside I whispered to Peter, "Break out the whiskey".

We sat in the tiny wardroom while Cecil explained that space had been booked in the dockyard at Bristol for 527's refit. Dockyard space on the south coast was not available.

Peter and I stood and clicked glasses. A romp around Land's End and into Bristol was just what the doctor ordered.

The drudgery of slogging back and forth to Normandy was now interrupted. Instead, a leisurely voyage without the restraints of an escort. Our "broken back" dictated minimum exposure to rough seas so I would decide when to be at sea or in a harbour.

Cecil deserved a reward and more whiskies were poured. He finally left clutching a bottle of gin for "wifey" — or so he claimed.

Two days later we set off in the early morning. By noon the Bill of Portland was off to starboard, not to be seen again for about three months. An unexpected diversion would delay our return.

We anchored for the night in the shelter of a lovely curving bay, formed by the ill-named Scabbacombe Head. It deserved better. Gentle hills with green valleys came down to a coastal path, leading to nearby Brixham.

Late walkers paused to stare at us from the cliffside. Stoker Lewis almost fell overboard with excitement when two girls mischievously unbuttoned their blouses and flashed their bosoms for a mini-second.

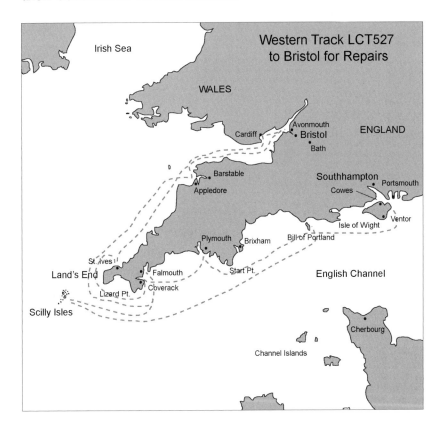

On rounding Start Point the following morning for a seventy mile run to Lizard Point we ran into stiff winds from the sou'west. I decided on caution and headed for Plymouth Harbour, just 20 miles away.

As we approached the breakwater an armed motor launch, like an alert guard dog, came snarling toward us, Aldis signal lamp demanding identification. We were flattered by their attention. Curtly ordering us to follow he went off toward the breakwater, tail wagging, at having foiled an attack by the German Navy, disguised as one of His Majesty's Landing Craft.

Inside the breakwater he now kindly directed us to a pier at the end of Drakes Island. With Raleigh, Frobisher and Hawkins the swashbuckling Drake is an integral part of Plymouth's history. It was from here they sailed to take on the Spanish Armada and "singe the King of Spain's beard".

As an important shipbuilding and military centre Plymouth had been targeted by the Luftwaffe. It was sad to see piles of rubble in the old city centre. Elsewhere, there were reminders of the city's history. Captain Cook's departure to the South Seas, convict ships to Australia and the Mayflower Pilgrims to a new life in America. William Bligh of the Bounty was baptised in St. Andrew's Church, now a pile of rubble from German bombs.

After three days I decided that we would continue our voyage. As we went through the breakwater, Peter, with a wink said, "We all enjoyed our stay in Plymouth and must thank the weatherman." I looked away. "No comment," I said.

Having left Plymouth later than planned I decided on one more stop before rounding Land's End. A five-hour run brought us to Coverack, a fishing port on the east side of the Lizard peninsula.

We anchored at the end of a sheltered bay. Inland were villages with enticing names, including Frenchman's

Creek, inspiration for Daphne du Maurier's novel of the same name.

I struggled with the temptation to stay for a few days to explore the area, described by du Maurier as "still and soundless, surrounded by trees, hidden from the eyes of man."

Peter too wanted to explore. His perspective was frivolous. He said, "A five-mile walk inland will bring us to 'Lower Bowells.' If time allows we can then linger awhile in nearby 'Little Nookie.'"

With an equally straight face I said that I had always been keen to visit 'Upper Sheepshagger.'[1]

"Is that so!" Peter said. "How keen?"

The next morning the sea was flat calm. There was no excuse for lingering and by 0830 we had rounded Lizard Point, on our way to Land's End. Regretfully we passed Penzance and Mousehole (pronounced 'Mozle") and continued around Land's End. Altering course to the Northeast we were abeam of St. Ives by midafternoon.

Wary of the almost unbroken line of cliff along the coast ahead I decided to spend the night in St. Ives. Since the turn of the century when fish reserves decreased dramatically St. Ives continued to attract artists. From our berth at the fishing pier we strolled to nearby streets There were paintings, sculptures and ceramics on view, some dating from the early 1920s.

---

[1]Fun names, attributed to Wodehouse et al. Actual British place names include: Blubberhouse, Blo Norton, Chew Magna, Lickey End, Nether Wallop, Powfoot, Potto, Sanahole, Seething, Sockburn, Titsey, Ugley, Whiterash, Wrangle, Yonder Bognie.

Peter returned aboard late in the evening and came by the wardroom to say "Good Night". I looked up from my book. "And where have you been Number One?" I said. He thought for a moment, "I was looking for the man from St. Ives with seven wives, to offer my help."

"Take a cold shower and get some sleep." I said. "We leave at 0600 hours for the run to Avonmouth."

Chapter 14

BED AND BREAKFAST ET CETERA

We waited 24 hours at Avonmouth for the right tide and an obligatory pilot to take us up the sinuous River Avon through a system of locks and into Bristol Dockyard.

Once there, no time was wasted and by next day the crew had, to their great delight, set off on a month's leave. I was touched when, individually, they all bade me farewell.

I had a drink with Petty Officer Bates and sent my regards to his wife Betty.

Stoker Lewis was known to his mates by the lower deck equivalent of "a ladies man", (an eight-letter word beginning with C). When he came by to say farewell I jokingly said "Now don't get into trouble with the ladies." He gave a knowing leer, saluted, and left. I knew that any female, without benefit of chastity belt or armed guard, was in jeopardy.

Peter did not leave until the following day. We had a farewell dinner at the Nova Scotia, a traditional dockside pub with seats by the lock.

I had decided to stay on in a nearby Bed & Breakfast and Peter was concerned about my welfare. I assured him that the B&B suited my plans, a base from which I could visit Pop and Mom Hart in Surrey or Uncle Hugh and Aunt Grace in Cambridgeshire. Knowing that Peter's first stop was the Isle of Wight I sent my regards to Sally and her father at the Folly Inn.

I had chosen my accommodation well, a large two-storey house on a dead-end street. For two pounds a week I had a second-floor bedroom with French doors, opening onto a small balcony, breakfast and laundry included.

My tenure of at least a month, instead of the usual week-end drop-ins, was welcomed by Nancy Bryson, my charming and attractive land-lady. Widowed by the disaster at Dunkirk she was determined "to get on with her life". I immediately felt at home and enjoyed her mischievous sense of humour.

Nancy encouraged informality. On meeting fellow guests on the wide staircase between floors we often sat on the steps for a chat and coffee. A large landing, halfway up, with a table and chairs invited lingering; the spacious sitting room on the ground floor was seldom used.

The first two weekends were with my dear friends in Surrey and Cambridgeshire. On each occasion when returning to Bristol I was given a prodigal's welcome, Nancy insisting on serving me breakfast in bed.

Remembering Maureen Dooley's suggestion of a country walk I arranged that she visit Bristol for a long weekend. Nancy gave her a room on the ground floor.

Using the B&B as a base we took day-long walks. On the first day we set off early for the twelve-mile walk to Bath. Choosing a path well away from the motorway we followed the course of the River Avon. Sunlight filtered through autumn tinted woods and dappled our leaf-strewn path.

Emerging on to a plain, Georgian buildings of pale gold Bath stone stood out on the city's elegant crescents.

There was much to be seen: hot spring baths created by the Romans, museums, sweeping vistas from the crescents. The buildings and streets were so harmonious that we lingered until late afternoon and returned to Bristol by bus.

The next day we crossed the 700-foot-long Clifton suspension bridge spanning the Avon Gorge. Continuing into the countryside beyond we chose a circular route that brought us back to Bristol in the late afternoon.

Maureen was departing on the afternoon of the third day. We spent the morning in the spacious garden in the rear of the B&B. Sitting closely together on a bench we became aware that we were holding hands. Looking ruefully at each other we withdrew our hands.

We spoke of this frankly and agreed that time was needed before our friendship could move into a more intimate dimension. The tendrils of our lost loves were still there, deep and encompassing and precluded other emotional commitments at this time. On parting we embraced and agreed to keep in touch.

Chapter 15

A CRUISE TO THE SCILLY ISLES

Repairs to our "broken back" completed and the crew on board we prepared for departure. There was a fond farewell from Nancy. I would not forget her special blend of hospitality.

We made our way down river to Avonmouth and on to Cardiff, twenty miles away. There was a delay in the obligatory compass adjustment and our departure was not until early on the third day. Fate had some surprises up her sleeve. We were not to see Portland for several weeks.

Rounding Bull Point by mid-afternoon we ran into heavy winds from the sou'west. I decided to take shelter in Appledore, just ten miles away.

Guarded by the shifting sands of Bideford Bar the approach to Appledore is tricky, even in calm weather. Now pounded by Atlantic rollers the roiled up mud and sands was most forbidding.

My alternative was to seek shelter around Hartland Point, about twelve miles to the west. Before altering course I detected the slight indication of a channel into Appledore, the outgoing waters of the River Taw.

Cautiously at first and then with more confidence we followed this into Appledore. It was with great relief that we tied up for the night at a pier, dating from Appledore's ship building past.

In the late afternoon of the following day Peter and I clambered to a hilltop above the village with views to the west. Lundy Isle, twenty miles away was indistinct in the cloudy overcast.

We were amazed to see a craft approaching from the direction of Bideford Bar. It wallowed along, at times hidden by the turbulent waters. As it neared we recognised it as a LCT Mark 4. We were relieved when it was safely in the channel.

Hurrying down the hill we saw the craft tying up alongside 527. Coming nearer we saw, to our amazement that it was LCT 801, with my friend and former commanding officer, Harvey "Nick" Nicholson.

We had not seen each other for almost a year and there was much to talk about. A celebration followed, with many whiskies and gin with orange. Nick explained that on completing minor repairs in Cardiff and having his compass adjusted, he was told of a Bahamian skipper passing through the day before. He knew that I was somewhere in the area.

Nick had another more compelling reason to seek shelter in Appledore. His scientist brother, David, was in Barnstaple just ten miles away. They hadn't seen each other for two years. The brother was involved in some covert wartime activity. I was never enlightened as to its nature or, why it took place in the wilds of Devon.

With day trips to Barnstaple, Westward Ho and other delightful destinations the days passed swiftly. The weather never seemed quite suitable for our onward voyage.

On about the tenth day Nick and I went to the hilltop to check on weather conditions. It was flat calm, the surface unbroken all the way to the horizon. "Well," I said, "what do you think?"

"I wouldn't want you to risk another *broken back*", Nick said with a smile, "but let's prepare to leave early in the morning." We went though the channel at first light. Nick in 801, as senior officer, led the way. The weather remained fair and we tied up in St. Ives for the night. The next day a leisurely run around Land's End brought us to Falmouth to be given some surprising instructions by the NOIC.[1]

Nick and I met with Captain Gordon, a genial RN four-striper who welcomed us into his orbit of command. He was intrigued that we wore shoulder flashes showing our countries: NEW ZEALAND and BAHAMAS. His orders were that we remain at Falmouth for a projected assignment which required two Mark 4 LCTs. He was not forthcoming about the timing or nature of the assignment. In the meantime we were to proceed to the harbour of nearby St. Mawes, a small attractive town on the Roseland Peninsula.

LCTs had a reputation for hard-lying and the captain seemed concerned for our comfort. "You will be tied up near the Victory Inn, a friendly pub," he said, "so relax and enjoy yourselves." I was not about to tell him that for the last two months I had been pampered beyond my expectations.

---

[1] Naval Officer In Command

Captain Gordon was right. We were embraced by the habitués of the Victory Inn—quite literally. On the first evening, while enduring a monologue from the local squire, Trelawney, on the joys of pheasant shooting, I saw Nick and Peter at a corner table, being chatted up by two local beauties. I caught Peter's eye and jokingly wagged an admonitory forefinger in his direction.

Nick and I spent the next day walking over Squire Trelawney's estate. Not having used our issue 45 revolvers in combat we took them ashore for practice shots. Rabbits and pheasants were plentiful. Having been denied a live German we spared the woodland creatures.

About ten days later Nick was summoned to Falmouth for a meeting with Captain Gordon. We were ordered to proceed to St. Mary's Isle, one of the Scilly Isles, about one hundred in number, located twenty-eight miles off Land's End. There we would take on a cargo of RAF tracking equipment, now made obsolete by our successes in Europe.

The Scilly Isles were known for beautiful beaches and mild climate and we set off eagerly. We soon found that it was not "the piece of cake" as first thought. With fifteen-feet tides and rocks and reefs lined up like armed guards, the Scillies are difficult to navigate, even in good weather. Numerous wrecks attest to their unfriendly nature. Halfway there the weather deteriorated. On approaching, we nervously made our way between St. Agnes Isle and St. Mary's Isle, each with its attendant rocks and reefs lurking just beneath the surface.

Having made it into a bay off Hugh Town on St. Mary's Isle we were hesitant about anchoring on an untrustworthy bottom, in weather that continued to worsen.

Close enough, to communicate by loud–hailer we decided to "dry out". The tide, at its highest, was beginning to ebb so we beached with our tank doors down and kedge anchors out. This assured us of at least twelve hours of safety during the night. By dawn the weather had improved.

We remained on the beach about 48 hours, adjusting our position slightly with each tide. In the meantime lorries with obsolete equipment were driven on board.

The weather continued to improve and on the third day, with less nail-biting than on arrival, we departed for Falmouth. Having unloaded our cargo we were released by Captain Gordon and continued, in company, east along the coast to Portland. On arriving, we tied up to a trot buoy. 801 left the next day for Portsmouth. I remained, subject to orders from NOIC Portland.

A flotilla of landing craft on a calm crossing. These are LCG's rather than the author's LCT. They are the same as the LCTs except that they have heavier armament..

Chapter 16

A FOGGY CROSSING

The Allies were now in possession of the port of Le Havre, at the mouth of the River Seine. We sailed there as a Flotilla, under command of Lieutenant John Sutcliffe, from whom I had inherited 527.

The outward voyage was without incident. The return to England was memorable.

Le Havre's recent capture had left its harbour in shambles. Remains of bombed ships obstructed the entrance and inner harbour. Entering or leaving was a nautical obstacle course.

Discharging cargo onto a dockside was difficult due to the great difference between high and low tide. Constant adjustment of our mooring ropes was necessary.

Having unloaded 527 there was a three-day delay before the projected return voyage. John Sutcliffe and I discussed the possibility of a quick trip to Paris which had been recently liberated. Had we gone we would have been in serious trouble.

Just before midnight on the third day we were alerted to an emergency departure for England at dawn. The Germans had succeeded in forcing a bulge in the Allied line and were headed in our direction. Later we learned that the enemy advance was halted by the Allies but by dawn we were on high alert and ready for sea.

With a total of 24 LCTs and some other ships it took a long time to navigate around the wreckage at the entrance and out to the assembly area.

Forming into two lines with two M.T.B.s[1] as escort, we set off. An hour into the voyage a fog descended upon us, so dense that, standing on the bridge, it was difficult to see the bow, just 150 feet away. All the other craft disappeared from view.

The convoy was in disarray. It was every man for himself. I quickly set up a plotting station in the wardroom. Our salvation would be dead-reckoning: the calculation of our changing position, based on estimated speed, distance covered and the course steered, with corrections for known currents.

I decided to head for Ventnor, a fishing village on the south-east coast of the Isle of Wight, about 80 miles away. Except for periodic plotting in the wardroom, Peter and I remained on the bridge throughout the voyage Extra look-outs were posted in the bows and on both sides amidship.

Ghostly noises, distorted by the fog, were sometimes heard from other craft. The occasional sound of fog horns, alerted us to the presence of other ships.

Toward the end of the day, if our plotting was correct, we were now somewhere near Ventnor or nearby Shanklin, seemingly confirmed by our lead-line which indicated

---

[1] Motor Torpedo Boats

between seven to ten fathoms. We anchored and during the night kept four-hour watches, involving most of the crew.

It was disturbing to hear strange unidentifiable noises, at irregular intervals. With dawn the fog lifted. We were less than half a mile from shore. A herd of cows grazing on a cliffside meadow, with occasional mooing and bawling, explained the strange noises in the night.

It was now urgent that we report our position to NOIC Portland. Not having a radio I went near an anchored destroyer and requested by semaphore that he pass our position on to Portland.

We were told of four other LCTs from our flotilla, anchored near Sandown, five miles away. One of these was Flotilla Leader Sutcliffe. Now reduced to five we teamed up, and arrived in Portland by mid-afternoon.

Of the 24 LCTs overtaken by fog, four had braved darkness and fog and were already in Portland. One had missed Portland Bill and went ashore on the East Devon coast near Sidmouth, with considerable damage. The other 14 craft straggled into Portland during the next 24 hours.

Chapter 17

V-E DAY

When in London I usually stayed at the Strand Palace Hotel. It suited my slender means and was conveniently near Trafalgar Square and Piccadilly Circus. Checking in there for a weekend in the spring of 1945, I ran into John Taylor, a fellow graduate of HMS King Alfred. We shared an interest in running. After graduation, a knee injury had denied John shipboard duty. Instead he was on shore duty at the Admiralty.

Over drinks and dinner I discovered that John was in the Admiralty Section that dealt with appointments. Lights flashed and bells clanged in my head. Maybe this was a chance for a few weeks in Nassau.

Usually wary of liqueurs after a bibulous dinner, I now ordered brandies. I spoke, almost tearfully, of my aged parents, terminally ill aunt, and brothers and sisters in Nassau. John was sympathetic.

The next morning I felt somewhat contrite about my obvious scheming and was astonished, three weeks later, to receive orders to join the Navy-run Contraband Control, in Port-of-Spain, Trinidad.

A gleeful phone call from John confirmed the appointment. The joker in the deck was that I be routed through Nassau, with a three-week vacation there. I would then continue on to Trinidad.

The orders were copied to NOIC Portland, with whom I met a day or so later. He had decided to send 527s crew on leave pending appointment of a new Commanding Officer. I suggested that a new First Lieutenant be appointed instead and that Peter be promoted to Commanding Officer. NOIC had met Peter and agreed that this was a sensible solution.

It was with mixed feelings that I took leave of the crew. We were an efficient team, tested by events of the past year, together enduring with good humour, the hard-lying discomforts of a LCT. I would take away fond memories.

Parting from Peter was more difficult. For a year he had been my right hand, always there when needed. We were close friends, with a mutual respect that kept intact the chain of command, while allowing camaraderie.

On the morning of my departure from Portland I climbed the stark and wind-battered hill above the harbour, to bid farewell to LCT 527.

To the north was the graceful bay of Weymouth and beyond, hazy with distance, the hills and valleys of Dorset. 527, now unmanned and forsaken, lay at a mooring below, the warhorse on which I had been tested, the focus of a year of wartime memories.

By the last week in April 1945 I was on a Pan Am seaplane, landing in Nassau Harbour. We taxied to the ramp at the Eastern parade, from which I'd departed three years earlier.

It all looked the same. St. Matthew's Church was glimpsed through giant silk-cotton tree branches, almond trees were shedding leaves and a horse-drawn carriage clip-clopped leisurely toward the city.

My mother and father were frail; the anxieties of four sons in the Navy and Air Force had hastened old age. My arrival gave them hope that my three brothers would also soon return.

It was a delight to meet my sister-in-law, Mary, brother Leonard's wife. My youngest brother Joe, twelve years old at my departure, was now a strapping fifteen-year-old.

I was content to stay at home with my family. They were eager to hear of my adventures, especially events that included my serving brothers.

My parents' failing health was of deep concern. My father died before I finally returned in 1946. I would be forever grateful to my friend John Taylor for "pulling the strings" that made my visit possible.

Seven days after my arrival Germany formally surrendered. Our family and friends, a party of about twenty, celebrated with a picnic on Cable Beach. A lot of rum was consumed. The distance of three thousand miles from war-torn England diluted the significance of this special day. For some it was merely an excuse for a party, for others it had profound meaning.

Mary, my sister-in-law, was ecstatic. Her husband Leonard, a prisoner-of-war in Germany, would now be released and his return home hastened. Others had similar personal reasons to celebrate.

I remember walking along the beach, trying to comprehend the profound implications of this day of victory. For a moment the events of the last three years, with cruel deaths and irreparable losses, crowded in on me. The warm, gentle

Bahamian sea, cloudless sky and nearby family and friends seemed illusory.

There were voices calling. Mary and my brother Joe were beside me, urging me to rejoin the party, and I realised how very fortunate I was to be at home.

In some deep recess of my being, I would forever imagine being in London on V-E Day, to share in the jubilation of victory, be one of a mighty rejoicing throng. To see those tiny figures, icons of our vast tribe, wave from a Buckingham Palace balcony, every half hour; to be frequently embraced by all and sundry.

Five decades after V-E Day I read "Deliverance", a moving account by talented writer Jean Hayworth.[1] As I read a half-century slipped away and I was in London on that memorable May Day — rejoicing and remembering.

Jean has generously allowed me to quote extensively from "Deliverance":

---

[1]Jean Hayworth joined the Royal Canadian Army Medical Corps in 1942 as a Lieutenant Nursing Sister. After several months she was posted to a hospital in Southern England. In April 1944 her Unit moved to Yorkshire to train for Operation Overlord. Shortly after D-Day Jean left from Portsmouth to land on Juno Beach in Normandy. Transferred to a Mobile Casualty Clearing Unit they followed the Canadian Army and Air Force through Belgium and into Holland. In London Jean met Flight Lieutenant Donald Hayworth, a Canadian Spitfire Pilot, also serving in the European Theatre. They were married on Christmas Eve 1944, attended by Jean's brother, Sandy Borland, who was killed in action the following day. Jean returned to England in January 1945 and served in No. 11 General Hospital until the War ended.

London, May 1945

For days there had been an air of anticipation hanging over all of England. Nowhere was it more palpable than in London on that lovely evening in early May of 1945. Don and I were up there on leave. We had spent three days revisiting our old haunts after nearly a year of service in the European Theatre of War. That evening we were in Regent Street standing at the curb, risking life and limb to dash into the road, hoping to flag down a taxi. Our plan was to go to the cinema in Leicester Square. Suddenly we were in luck as one veered into the curb to pick us up.

The film was less than memorable and after a hurried discussion we decided to leave. Without warning, the screen went black and the heavy curtains chugged slowly across the stage. There was a sudden buzz of speculation, which was silenced as a man at centre stage, spotlighted there, slowly raised his hands. Then he stepped forward, flung out his arms and shouted, "It's over, the war is over." We sat there in stunned disbelief. Then the houselights came up and the crowd, almost as one stood, and slowly left the theatre. People were quietly talking together, scarcely daring to believe, as the realisation of what had been said began to sink in.

Brilliant sunshine greeted us outside and for a moment we were dazzled. Then we stared, watching as the square rapidly filled up with people. They were streaming in from every doorway, every lane, very street and all with the same purpose — to share the jubilation of this moment. The thought of getting in a taxi was laughable. There were several marooned in the crowd, their drivers having abandoned them to join in the celebration. We decided to join the growing throng and try to make our way up Coventry Street to Piccadilly to see what was happening there. It was a slow walk, as a continuing number of people were joining us, all with the same purpose in mind. The people at times overwhelmed us asking where we were from and offering their effusive thanks for our service to their country until it became embarrassing. Never have I been embraced by so many total strangers. It was so heart-warming and moving to us. As we neared Piccadilly, the sound became more and more tumultuous. It was evident that a great crowd had gathered there as we came to the broad expanse of the great ring.

I was too short to see over the heads of most of the crowd and Don, hanging tight to my arm, kept a running commentary into my ear. At one point, he gestured towards a bus that was marooned in the crowd like so many others. On its top, there was a young soldier prancing up and down, doing an impromptu strip-tease, much to the hilarity of the crowd. He was flinging bits of his uniform over their heads and they were roaring with every one of his movements. Suddenly we were pulled into a group of conga dancers, snaking its long line throughout the whole area and enveloping everyone in its way. That was such fun and we found ourselves at one point circling the sandbag base of the old statue of Eros, which had long since been removed for safekeeping.

Around and around we went, finally able to extricate ourselves. As we moved through the crowd, the light began to dim and I looked up to see that the long lavender twilight of an English summer evening was almost over. To my surprise, I found that we had reached the west side of the ring. We were now within walking distance of our ultimate goal, "The Rendezvous Club". It was a club for Allied fighter pilots and we'd hoped to meet our friends there for a hilarious evening.

We were almost there when a brilliant light sprang up on the far side of the road. We stared in amazement watching the light shining on the fluttering Allied flags someone had strung up along the corner of a building opposite us. There was a hush and a strong male voice suddenly began to sing "When the lights come on again, all over the world". He was joined by hundreds of voices. We stood there, in our own silence. I saw Don's lips move — "I wish..." and I knew he was thinking of all the boys who would not be coming back, our two brothers among them. We stood there staring at that strong beam of hope lighting up the sky after almost six long years of darkness. Our eyes were fixed on that beam, our hearts filled with mingled sadness and great joy and pride, our bodies locked together in a tight embrace lost in a moment in time.

Chapter 18

THE BEGINNING OF THE END

The end of the war in Europe was celebrated in England and America on 8 May, known thereafter as V- E Day. Surrender by pockets of resistance continued until 11 May, with a final capitulation at Heligoland.

Euphoria in England was tempered by the commitment to stand with the United States in the Pacific. The Royal Navy supported the United States' Navy, and British forces still slogged it out in steaming jungles.

But inevitably a winding-down began in many areas of the war effort. On arrival in Port of Spain I found that Contraband Control was already anticipating closure, its surveillance of passing neutral ships now decidedly perfunctionary.

Captain Benbow RNR,[1] our C.O., looked forward to continuation of his retirement, from which he had volunteered for the post of NOIC Contraband Control, Trinidad.

I was one of the Captain's six officer assistants with little to do. Our shared sentiment was that we were now on an all expense paid holiday, courtesy of "George."[2]

---

[1] Royal Navy Reserve

[2] King George VI

Our base on the waterfront looked out to an anchorage, to which ships — usually Portuguese or Spanish — were escorted by a Navy vessel.

We preferred to board Spanish or Portuguese passenger ships, on their way to South America. Our launch took us alongside. A charade would follow.

Welcomed by uniformed personnel we were installed in first-class accommodation for a night or two. A cocktail party followed our arrival, attended by lovely senoritas on their way to Buenos Aires or Rio de Janeiro. Any thoughts of a tryst at midnight on the afterdeck were quelled by fierce looks from their chaperones.

The only find that I recall was a stamp collection, said to be of considerable value. It was not confiscated.

The job was so obviously a sinecure that, with Captain Benbow's blessing, I became involved in local athletics, arranging friendly field events: Navy competing with the Trinidad Police in running, jumping, etc.

We put together a Navy Rugby Team to play against local teams. Our star player, Tim Otway, a fellow officer from Tobago, was a talented wing forward.

There was time to explore. We climbed Cerro Aripo, at 3085 feet the island's highest peak, and visited spectacular Maracas Falls. Soon after my arrival I was taken to the beautiful beach at Macaripe with its extensive grove of graceful coconut palms. It became our favourite destination for a day's outing.

A pleasant memory was meeting Lieutenant Brian Moody, an Englishman married to Eileen Saunders from Nassau. I was always welcome at their apartment, enlivened by

Madeline, a delightful toddler. Sixty years later I remember with gratitude their hospitality to a fellow Bahamian.

The orders to discontinue Contraband Control operations finally came through. Tim Otway and I were given passage to England on an aircraft carrier. The C.O., who never smiled, informed us that we would be working our passage. This was fair enough, but he then arranged that, as Watch Keeping Officers, we would always be on the midnight watch. Tim and I decided that it was his way of giving his regular officers some respite from night watches, at our expense.

At 0200 hours on one of my watches, the C.O.'s grouchy voice called through the voice pipe to the bridge, giving me a blast because the helmsman had strayed a degree off course. This occasionally happened to the most skilful helmsman. If not immediately corrected, the OOW[3] would intervene.

I imagined the C.O. staring at his cabin compass and relishing any excuse to tear a strip off a strange junior officer.

When I left the ship I gave him a dirty look and an imaginary fore-finger gesture. I decided never to set foot on his ship again.

---

[3] Officer of the Watch

On arrival in Southampton, I was directed to RNB[4] Portsmouth. Installed there in the Officers' Quarters I awaited instructions. Several weeks went by.

With permission to travel—subject to a contact phone number—I visited friends in Surrey and Cambridgeshire, with an occasional foray into London. My friends were welcoming and generous, but there were self-imposed limitations to my visits.

During the three months following V-E Day, England's forces were fully committed to helping the United States in the Pacific War. In August, the atom bomb brought a final end to war. England was now faced with the daunting task of releasing millions of serving men and women into an impoverished economy. For this transition to be orderly the remainder of 1945 and several months into 1946 would be required.

Like most hostilities-only overseas servicemen, I found it tedious to wait around for demobilisation and passage home. I was not unusually vocal, but some senior officer must have heard me complain. Inexplicably, I was ordered to report to the officer in charge at Whale Island for a six-week gunnery course.

Wartime Whale Island was known for rigorous discipline and a demanding curriculum. I arrived to find a sea-change. After six years, with war no longer a spur, the instructors were disenchanted. We found the course relaxing and somewhat entertaining, albeit a waste of time.

Lectures were few; limited to one or two a day, four days a week. We soon found that attendance at practical sessions — dismantling guns and the mysteries of high calibre guns — was voluntary. There were no exams. In short, it was a farce

---

[4] Royal Naval Barracks

intended to keep us and any "hostility-only" instructors occupied until demobilisation.

In the area of accommodation the course was noteworthy. With five other officers I was given quarters on Her Majesty's Yacht *Victoria and Albert,* moored to a nearby pier. On this craft Queen Victoria and her consort, Albert, had crossed to Osborne, her Isle of Wight estate, and, no doubt, voyaged to the Thames.

At the Queen's death in 1901 it became the Royal Yacht for the reigning monarch. Its outward grandeur had faded but some effort had been made to maintain the interior. We each had our own cabin.

Some of us had access to Queen Victoria's loo. It was quite ordinary, except for a velvet cover on the seat. We assumed the cover had been replaced in the intervening fifty years, but small clouds of dust indicated otherwise.

Inevitably, this was the cause of great ribaldry. One of our group irreverently ventured that should our future accomplishments not be recognised by a Royal Knighthood we could at least claim having sat on the same loo as Her Majesty Victoria, Queen of The United Kingdom and Empress of India.

Now back in RNB Portsmouth I sought relief from the tedium of enforced idleness. On a visit to Uncle Hugh at Fordy Farm in Cambridgeshire I learned a lot about sugar beet and, more importantly, felt useful when tramping over the fields with Mr. Slack, the foreman.

Mr. Slack taught me the most efficient way of crossing the many ditches which criss-crossed the flat fen country. I rationalised that knowing how to jump a ditch or grow a sugar beet might be useful one day. You never know.

On the pig farm Mr. Slack showed me the best way to encourage a sow to succumb to the advances of a boar. I took note. You never know.

In due course, I was appointed to the Training Staff at HMS Warrington, located — you've guessed it — in Warrington, an establishment engaged in turning recruits into sailors.

I assumed that, as hostility-only sailors and veterans flooded into civvy street, their Lordships found it necessary to maintain the Navy at a certain strength.

My job had little to do with the actual training of sailors. At the end of every week or two about a hundred Ordinary Seamen would be turned out. It was my job, with the assistance of a Petty Officer or leading Seaman, to deliver them to a destination, usually Cardiff. From there, given an official receipt, I returned to Warrington, unless tempted to stay for the rest of the weekend.

We traveled by train, with changes at stations along the way. Sometimes individuals would wander off to nearby shops or pubs. If a head count twenty minutes before train departure came up short, panic would ensue while we rounded up the stragglers.

At the beginning of each journey I would appoint half a dozen likely assistants, usually the class leaders. This seemed to help.

As I had little to do between Monday and Friday, I appointed myself instructor to the Wren's Basketball Team. I knew very little about basketball but the Wrens were eager, and we all learned quickly. It was entertaining and my team became good enough to take on the men's team. I have a photograph to prove it.

Wren's team standing. Men's team kneeling. Author kneeling at extreme right.

There was time for short trips, the most memorable to the seaside at Morecambe. It was winter-time and hardly anyone was about, but I enjoyed walking along its promenade.

At the turn of the previous century Morecambe was one of Britain's premier seaside resorts, but was overtaken by Blackpool. Its natural attributes surpass anything offered by Blackpool. Standing on the promenade, muffled against the cold, looking across the vast bay to the distant peaks of Cumbria, I felt elated. But I soon sought the warmth of a tea room before returning to Warrington.

Chapter 19

HOMEWARD BOUND

Breathes there the man, with soul so dead
Who never to himself hath said,
This is my own, my native land.
Whose heart hath ne'er within him burned
As home his footsteps he hath turned
From wandering on a foreign strand!

Sir Walter Scott

Late in the spring of 1946 I received an Embarkation Notice. I was to be in Southampton three weeks later for passage to New York on the *S.S. Queen Mary.*

There was time for a farewell weekend with Mom and Pop Hart in Surrey. Their son, my friend Tony, was there with his fiancée, Penelope, who lived nearby.

Three years before when leaving the doomed *HMS Beverley,* Tony had taken me to meet his parents, Cecil and Kitty. They were welcoming. *Bargates,* their lovely home, on a hill overlooking the village of Bramley became my 'home away from home,' 'Mom' and 'Pop' Hart my surrogate parents. I would be forever grateful.

Thence to Fordy Farm, near Ely, in Cambridgeshire for a final visit with Auntie Grace and Uncle Hugh. Dear gentle Auntie, still grieving for her Jack, lost in the Great War;

Uncle, the quintessential country gentlemen, equally courteous to labourer or aristocrat.

It was a weekend and we walked to the little church in Barway for the Sunday service. Our path led along the shores of a small lake and through a green tunnel formed by overhanging branches of ancient elms, evoking memories of Annabel.

The last week was spent in London. I was obliged to take a routine medical exam which preceded demobilisation. Although the waiting room was crowded, the procedure was orderly. The overworked doctor was witty. After the usual prodding, bending over, peering into various apertures, he pronounced me fit. I asked, "Do you mean 'fit to be tied' or 'fit to kill'?" "No," he said, "fit as a fiddle."

I was surprised to learn that some educational benefits might be available to ex-servicemen, even though England's economy was in tatters. An appointment for an interview was granted.

It was quite short. A pompous individual with a large nose and a little moustache questioned me, as was expected. "What do you want to study?" "Why?" etc. In response to "Where are you from?" I replied, "The Bahamas." He sniffed, "Oh yes – a colonial, what!" I should have said, "Yes, you insufferable prig." Instead, I waited for his further comment.

Riffling through some papers he finally said, "The best I can offer is a six-months course in 'agricultchar'". I knew this really meant extra help on a farm. I explained that this was not what I had in mind. He was not convinced and said, "Well Thompson, it may not be your 'cup of tea', but it could be of benefit to the colony from which you came."

I gave up and left, hoping his Pinocchio nose would drop off. Then he couldn't look down it at 'lesser mortals' and his disdainful sniffle would be cured. He should also shave his ridiculous moustache.

A delightful surprise awaited me when I boarded *S.S. Queen Mary.* My friend, David Lightbourn and his lovely bride, Joan, were also on board. Our cabins were adjoining and we began a voyage-long celebration.

In addition to many servicemen, there were a thousand nurses and a thousand war brides destined for Halifax or New York.

We soon had many friends. Jacques, a French Canadian Army officer and Barbara and Mary Jane from New Brunswick, joined our group. The weather was fine throughout the voyage and a section of sheltered deck became our base. There was a joyous mood throughout the ship: we had survived and were returning to our homes.

On the first day out, in the late afternoon, I made my way to the stern and gazed eastward. England was already below the horizon.

I knew that this island in the North Sea would forever be the focal point of endearing memories: its country lanes, the call of larks high in the sky, wind crossing a wheatfield, the shriek of seagulls in a calm harbour after a stormy voyage — its wondrous people: Churchill's "We shall never surrender", a Lancashire bus conductress saying 'There you are, luv", new friends who became family, trusty shipmates.

Twilight gently deepened into darkness and the horizon merged with sea and sky.

As I stared at the churning wake I realised that my war service – all of it, the good and the bad, the joy and the sadness – was woven into the fabric of my being, as I now faced a new beginning.

THE END

EPILOGUE

O that 'twere possible
After long grief and pain
To find the arms of my true love
Around me once again!…

Ah yes! That it were possible
For one short hour to see
The souls we loved, that they might tell us
What and where they be ….

Tennyson

A fishing trip has been arranged and the old man awaits his granddaughters. He smiles as he looks to the south and west; scattered fleecy white clouds, bright sunlight, the sea's surface gently ruffled by a soft wind. "Perfect for turbot fishing," he thought.

On his patio, a golden silence, sounds from passing boats hushed by distance. A giant madeira casts benevolent shade, a dove alights briefly and, head on one side, peers at the old man, an inquisitive curly-tailed lizard inches nearer.

High aloft, several frigate birds defy gravity and, wings motionless, glide across the arc of sky. As if aware of his gaze one of these tips its wings into a steep downward spiral. The old man has seen this before and its symbolism is clear. He smiles, "Not yet, prophetic bird! NOT! QUITE! YET!"

The rocking chair is comfortable, he slept little the night before, his eyes close and he drifts downward, "full fathom five", to that realm where the lost ones await, in silent unmoving ranks. They are unchanged, forever young, untouched by sixty years of history, unaware that they were denied the chance to study, to marry, to make a home, to have children, to watch a garden grow. It is he who has grown old.

Unknowingly, they joined the lost ones of The Great War, of whom Rupert Brooke wrote:

> Blow out, you bugles, over the rich Dead!
> There's none of these so lonely and poor of old,
> But, dying, has made us rarer gifts than gold.
> These laid the world away, poured out the red
> Sweet wine of youth; gave up the years to be
> Of work and joy, and that unhoped serene
> That men call age; and those who would have been,
> Their sons, they gave, their immortality."

There is a stirring, like wind across a wheat field, the ranks part and Annabel appears, moving just above the ground, as she seemed to do in life. She is nearby, blonde curls in disarray. He reaches out but cannot touch her.

She speaks, "Please, may I come fishing too?" "Of course, my darling," he says. "You'll be there. And after fishing we'll pick seagrapes."

A hand on his shoulder and the old man awakens. His granddaughters are waiting. "We're ready gran'pa, time to go." He stands and gazes at their youthful, smiling faces and rejoices at his good fortune. "I'm ready." he says.

They turn away and then pause. "Was there someone here?", one says. "We thought we heard voices." He looks into their bright eyes and smiles, "No, my dears," he said, "it was just the rustle of leaves in the wind."